Make
Wealth
Happen

Matthews, Craig E. 1960-

For information contact info@makewealthhappen.ca or 403.543.1511

Editor: C. Nanton
Artwork-layout-design: R.A.S.

To order this book in quantity, please contact the distributor:
> Inspire Media
> John Cordova
> National Sales Manager
> Tel: (702) 493-1789
> E-Mail: john@inspiremedia.biz
> Website: www.inspiremedia.biz

Published by: *Motivated Publishing Ventures*

ISBN: 0-9736187-6-0
Printed in Canada and U.S.A.

First Edition April 2005

Foreword

David Irvine

The philosopher, Eric Hoffer, once wrote,

"In times of change learners inherit the earth, while the learned find themselves beautifully equipped to deal with a world that no longer exists."

If you reflect for a moment on the past decade and envision the next ten years, you will recognize that the world in which most of us grew up is no longer with us. While there are many "learned" people who are in denial about the changes, you have this book in your hand; you are, undoubtedly a "learner" who is aware of the fundamental transformation that surrounds us at home and at work. And no more profound revolution surrounds us than our understanding of - and our relationship with - wealth.

No one makes this new perception of wealth clearer than Craig Matthews. He has turned me into a "learner" in the field of wealth creation, management, and preservation. For more than twenty years I have been a leader's navigator - inspiring and guiding leaders in all capacities to authentically connect with themselves and those they serve in order to amplify their impact in the world.

I first met Craig in 1998 when I made a presentation to a room full of his successful clients. Since that time I have come to know and respect Craig's wisdom and perspective. He is a leader who is helping people create a living and make a life. I have preached for years that living simply means living your life in alignment with your core values. What I have learned from Craig is that until you get a handle on this thing called wealth, you cannot live simply - or have lasting meaning in your life. Craig's inspiration, insightful philosophy, and practical processes for getting a grip on wealth in life have significantly changed my view of financial freedom, and of wealth creation and preservation. I am gifting this book to my young daughters as they prepare to live in the New World economy.

To thrive in this New World economy we will need to rethink the whole notion of wealth, retirement, and financial freedom. According to Craig, wealth is not financial, retirement is an outdated notion, and you can no longer count on your investment portfolio for financial freedom. All these are insights well worth considering. Real wealth, Craig ascertains, is created through our Five Wealth Assets - health, time, wisdom, relationships, and reputation. His practical philosophy will empower you to take control of your financial future, independent of the economic or political landscape.

Like me, you will enjoy this book. Philosophically, it affirms the responsibility each of us has to our own financial future. Money won't buy you happiness, but it will buy you options, and there is nothing wrong with a broad spectrum of choices in life.

This book goes far beyond analyzing money. It taps into the very meaning of life - creating what matters most to each of us by addressing the creation of capital in all areas of life. In this increasingly complex world, this book is for everyone who is committed to creating a predictable, sustainable future.

David Irvine, Author
Simple Living In A Complex World: A Guide To Balancing Life's Achievements
Becoming Real: Journey To Authenticity
Accountability: Getting a Grip on Results

$$5 \times 3 = \text{results}$$

5 wealth assets x 3 success ingredients = results

How Wealth Happens

Acknowledgements

I would like to thank my many clients who have made my journey a happy one. Each family that I work with has their own unique set of philosophies and values from which I'm able to learn each day.

Also, thanks to my team at The Wealth Strategists, my financial planning firm. Gayle, Gail, Aaron and Dean, you each add a different dimension to my life. Your patience, understanding and contribution are appreciated.

I would like to thank my wife of 20 years, Trudy White-Matthews. Trudy, thank you for keeping me on track and challenging all my ideas and thoughts. Your insights and questions truly PROVOKE me to strive to be a better person. You are a true-life partner.

Finally, my almost four-year-old son, Luca. Luca, you have no idea what you add to the enjoyment of my life. Your innocence is refreshing and your enthusiasm contagious. You make me feel young. This book is dedicated to you. My wish is for you to fully understand true wealth and to be able to maintain your innocence and enthusiasm throughout your lifetime.

Trudy and Luca, you are my greatest assets.

Thank you.

Table of Contents

A Note to my Readers

Thank you for engaging in my concepts by reading this book.

My hope with this book is to ultimately challenge your current way of thinking about wealth, and have you look at ways of expanding the definition to suit you. I will suggest that most of what we have learned about wealth up to now is just not relevant to the way the world works today.

More importantly I will share with you a combination of factors within your control that are the levers that directly influence the wealth that you achieve. I will cover three key concepts:

> Your wealth definition
> The Five Wealth Assets
> The Wealth Equation

Enjoy the read, and welcome to the new world of wealth.

Craig Matthews
info@makewealthhappen.ca

I would truly like to hear from you regarding these ideas.

Introduction

Almost everyone has heard one of the many versions of the story of the Holy Grail. It is one of the most romanticized legends about the relentless pursuit of self-transformation and personal liberation.

Despite the variety of interpretations of the nature and aspect of the Grail, what remains constant is the power inherent in the Grail - that promise of renewal or perhaps even the means of attaining immortality. Yet with such implied promise there is a constant nature of unworthiness in the stories of the Grail. Even the finest and most courageous proved unworthy. Only the pure were said to have been able to approach the Holy Grail; anyone else would simply see it disappear before his or her eyes. The Quest for the Holy Grail continues.

Question: Will you be happy when you find the Grail?

Wealth is today's version of the Holy Grail - that elusive concept that we mostly equate with having pots and pots of money. There are some that say the only way to get real money is to inherit it - or win the lottery! Yet many lottery winners have lost everything they won within a few years of receiving it. And many people who been "given" their fortunes and not had to create it themselves do not have the skills to maintain it or grow it, in fact there is lots of evidence that many children of the third and fourth generation are well on their way to decimating the money their parents and grandparents worked hard to amass.

As a Certified Financial Planner working with entrepreneurs and corporate executives, I have come to the conclusion that wealth is not created by investing in the stock market, purchasing an insurance policy or even by paying yourself first. (I realize many of you may have gone back and re-read that sentence, and yes, I really said that. I am a financial services professional challenging the promises constantly held out by the financial industry to entice clients.) The truth is there is no financial formula for investing your money that will create the kind of wealth you likely dream of having. This is an important point to clarify, as it is one of the first commonly held myths that I challenge. The financial tools I mentioned above do not drive wealth building. They are very important tools, but they are for the preservation of financial assets to protect your hard earned funds from taxation, inflation, death and disability. Very seldom do these strategies or products actually create wealth.

I am but one voice going in the opposite direction, and I urge you to consider this. The companies that provide financial products have spent decades and large fortunes training you to think of those products as wealth creators. I know it takes a second to reprogram that point of view. What you need to understand first and foremost is that YOU create the wealth before it even can be placed into one of these financial products.

I have rarely seen evidence that someone has created and sustained wealth by investing in the stock market (yes, there are exceptions, and they really are the minority); the same is true for great insurance products. What I have seen is people with wealth using these products and services to preserve and protect the wealth they have acquired through other means. Which is exactly what they are designed for. To be clear, I respect the financial products and their usability as a preservation tool, I take issue with their promise of wealth creation.

In fact, the secret to making wealth happen is not simply found in the pursuit of the dollar, but rather in the character you have and that you use as you create your wealth.

Each of us possesses five assets - what I call the Five Wealth Assets - that are the core of all wealth creation.

What follows in these pages is an explanation of how wealth is created through the Five Wealth Assets that each of us possesses - Health, Time, Wisdom, Relationships and Reputation. An explanation of the secret to the Holy Grail - that we hold the path to the Grail inside us. Have you ever thought that you might not have what it takes to be wealthy, because in spite of everything you have done, wealth has been elusive? I believe that through focus and planning, you can achieve that elusive Grail, wealth, however that may look to you.

In this volume, I want to help you use your what you already have at your disposal to make wealth happen for you.

Chapter 1

Understanding Wealth

In this chapter I am going to share with you the foundational concepts of this book. We will first explore what this seemingly simple yet elusively attainable idea of wealth is. Any book that purports to teach you how to create wealth has no value unless it first creates a thorough understanding of what wealth is and how we in North America relate to wealth in the twenty first century.

There are four precepts I'd like to propose to you:

1. Your definition of wealth is yours and yours alone.

Before you can create wealth, you must understand it; before you can understand it, you must define it. What is wealth? Webster's dictionary defines wealth as:

1. much money or property; riches; large possessions of money, goods or land; great abundance of worldly goods; affluence; opulence.
2. a large amount of something; an abundance, as a wealth of ideas.
3. valuable products contents or derivatives.

(Webster's Dictionary, 8th edition)

While the dictionary may lay it out clearly, each of us still has a very personal interpretation of what wealth looks like. What is the magic number? Perhaps it is not a number but it is about having time to be with family and friends? What does wealth mean to you? And which of the components best describe your picture of wealth? Because we all have different measures and markers for wealth, our definitions are as different and unique as each of us are different and unique.

2. We all start from the same spot.

We all start out with the same assets. I know, I can hear you shouting "That's not so!" This is another one of those myths I am challenging you on. And I know you're thinking about those who were born with the proverbial silver spoon in their mouths — the second and third generation Eaton, Weston, Stronach, Thompson, Irving, Kennedy, Rockefeller, Getty, all the others who experience the benefits of financial wealth merely by virtue of who their parents were. But I'm not talking about assets in terms of money — I'm talking about the personal, human, non-financial assets we acquire through our lifetime that equip us to make wealth happen as it fits our definition.

When I think of this precept, I am struck by the pertinence of a line I heard recently "It is not what you are born to be, it is about what you have in you to be."

3. Wealth rewards habits.

This one is fairly straightforward. It is about more than doing, it is doing things well, and smartly. It is about creating an environment that sets you up for success.

We have all heard stories of people who rise to the top of success in their field, then fall. Men and women who create empires, only to lose it all and start again - many have built their successes time after time. Wealth is not only created by, it is preserved through, confidence, having goals and vision, and acquiring knowledge, and only those who are true to these habits created on the way to their picture of wealth will be able to maintain, preserve, and make greater their success.

4. Everyone is successful in his or her own world.

If we each have our own definition of wealth and we each follow our own unique habits and path to creating that wealth, we will have success.

Your current habits equal your current results. This is another concept I'm going to challenge you with; you are one hundred percent accountable for your results. Your level of success is exactly how you behaved it. Your ideal form of success and corresponding wealth may be out of alignment with your actual situation, but your habits or behaviours are always related to your results, like it or not.

And more importantly, success is not comparative. No one else can determine your level of success. It's interesting how we factor in thinking about how we "ought" to or "should not" define our lives and success. In fact, our definition of success is often wrapped around our perception of what others think. Yet our degree of success can only be measured against someone else's achievement if each of us has had the same set of circumstances and the same set of goals.

The good news is that your success is only limited to your thinking and habits - and you can make that as big and as unique as you like. You are not restricted to someone else's worldview.

What is Wealth?

How do you define wealth?

Ask a room full of people to define wealth, and you will get an array of answers. It reminds me of the story of the blind men asked to describe what an elephant looks like. The analogy is this: there are four blind men who discover an elephant. Since the men have never encountered an elephant, they grope about, seeking to understand and describe this new phenomenon. One grasps the trunk and concludes it is a snake. Another explores one of the elephant's legs and describes it as a tree. A third finds the elephant's tail and announces that it is a rope. And the fourth blind man, after discovering the elephant's side, concludes that it is, after all, a wall.

Each in his blindness is describing the same thing: an elephant. Yet each describes the same thing in a radically different way.

This is like wealth — the definition is elusive — and it is only what is true for you. Some of the world's most successful men and women consider themselves not wealthy enough; and some of the people who live near the poverty level consider themselves hugely wealthy in terms of spirit, and family relationship. Take for instance first generation immigrants from the Philippines or Nepal. I know people in these communities who vividly remember what they have left behind and are grateful for new beginnings and the ability to send even small amounts of money home to help their families. The people in these communities that I know are rich in spirit, hopeful for their future and truly understand the value of family and community. These people have great wells of internal personal wealth in the absence of external material wealth.

No one can tell us what wealth is or define it for us — although the media certainly tries to paint a picture of idealized material wealth that many people have bought into.

The truth is there is no definition of wealth. Remember Webster's definition? An abundance of something.

But what is that something?

As no two people are the same so goes the definition of wealth, no two definitions are the same. For some wealth is defined as a specific monetary amount. I have a friend who has decided that when he is debt free and has ten thousand dollars per month coming in, he will be wealthy. And I have a client who maintains that a liquid bank account of one million dollars will declare his arrival at the doorstep of wealth. One articulate client describes wealth as the freedom to make the choices I want to make. In many cases, money is implied but there is no magic number to aim for. Even the individuals who identify wealth with money cannot agree on what amount to use in the definition.

Others rank their family as their number one asset. They declare that wealth is time to spend with family as needed, as desired. Wealth is being able to rush to a loved one's bedside in the event of an accident or illness without caring about the financial consequences. Wealth is being able to attend or send your children to the post secondary institution of your choice (in some cases, the one that's farthest away from home!) Wealth is having the number of children you want, not the number you can afford. Wealth is healthy, happy relationships with immediate and extended family members. Wealth is making sure that everyone in the family is secure.

I have a client who says, "Wealth is being able to compete in a triathlon on two weeks' notice." Just think about what that means. To pick up and go on short notice means that your work can manage without you — go on functioning in your absence and thrive. To enter any triathlon anywhere in the world means you have sufficient discretionary income — spending money — to pay for travel, accommodations, someone to support you in the race, transporting your equipment, entry fees… And it means that you have had sufficient time, energy and commitment to train every day in order to be fit and ready for a competition in two weeks' time. That definition of wealth is so much more than just money in the bank. It's a mindset about what wealth means — it's lifestyle.

Everyone has a different definition.

So if there is no singularly common definition, no set monetary amount, why are North Americans so focused on a financial definition of wealth while they sacrifice health, relationships, wisdom and reputation in search of the Money Grail?

Could it be as I have already asserted that the media and the purveyors of financial services and products have us believing that by investing in the mutual funds or purchasing an insurance policy we are building wealth?

You've seen the commercials advertising the "save now, retire at age 55" theory. Perhaps you've imagined yourself on this beach, or on that golf course — is that your definition of wealth? Or maybe you prefer the promise of continued income from the investment of mutual funds because it follows sound economic theory.

If everyone defines wealth differently, why is it that we listen to the media and manufactures of products to define it for us?

One theory is that we equate money with happiness. The media hypes wealthy individuals as role models. We see the glamorous life they live, the toys, the traveling, yet we know nothing about their private lives except what we read in the tabloids. I submit that, in fact, these individuals have no more happiness than you or I do — and with their celebrity status they may even have less. Having had the opportunity to work directly with hundreds of "high net worth" individuals, I find it interesting that these and others who define wealth as a number never really feel or consider themselves to be wealthy. Although many would say happiness is having one million dollars in the bank, the truth is financial wealth is not an emotion — it lives in the concrete, not in the affect. Financial wealth can only provide things that trigger emotions. So even with that million dollars in the bank, many financially wealthy individuals still feel a sense of insecurity and a fear of failure, and worry about family and health. It is not a panacea and it does not remove the other worries.

This is key: you must create your own picture of wealth for you and your family. Only then will you be in a position to control your future.

Your Five Wealth Assets

What are your Wealth Assets?

When asked this question most individuals would answer their house, their retirement pool, possibly their car, other real estate or even their business.

I would call these your financial assets. Most individuals confuse their Wealth Assets with financial assets. This is no mistake on our part - that's what we've been told, and sold. We have always been told our assets are our homes, our businesses, and our retirement accounts. And to some extent that is correct but the true question is, "What are your WEALTH assets?" What are the assets you use to acquire those financial assets? Wealth Assets and financial assets should not be confused.

Remember earlier we talked about how we all start at the same place. This is what I was referring to. Everyone starts out working with the same Wealth Assets.

Think about the assets that are yours alone to leverage and maximize or fritter away. The assets that you have total control and ownership over. What are the assets that actually make wealth happen?

Here are your five Wealth Assets:

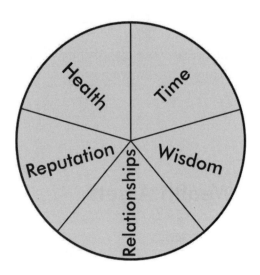

God willing, each of us arrives in this world with health and time. As we grow, we gain wisdom, we establish relationships and we develop our reputation. Each of us has the same material to work with; it's a level playing field. I hear you saying that some of us are born into privilege, and some into poverty. I submit that regardless of our socio-economic status, we still possess an equal potential to achieve. Otherwise, how do you explain the rags to riches stories? Few of those stories have anything to do with lotteries or luck - most report hard work, determination and recognition of opportunity.

The difference is how we view and manage these assets. Everyone manages them differently, according to their definition of wealth and success, and this creates the uniqueness in our success and in society.

This explains why some individuals can go from poverty to financial wealth. Take Oprah Winfrey for example: a poor girl who grew up in a deprived environment, suffering abuse — an environment that we would not expect to foster success. Yet today she is one of the most influential and successful individuals in North America. She was the first African-American woman to become a billionaire, and has committed her life to informing, empowering and enlightening women throughout the world. Oprah has always said she believes less in luck and more in preparedness meeting opportunity. That is all about her proactively managing her Five Wealth Assets.

Another example is Stephen Hawking, the great scientist. When he was 21 years old, Stephen was diagnosed with ALS, a motor neuron disease that causes the muscles to progressively become weaker. At that time he realized that even if he were to die sooner rather than later, he could at least make a contribution to society. And with each new restriction to his abilities, he created new coping mechanisms, used new technologies, and today has contributed brilliantly to the field of theoretical physics. Even having lost the ability to speak, he is able to give presentations, research and write, and his insight is sought after all over the world.

How did he do it? He managed his Five Wealth Assets. While health was an obvious issue, he did not let it stop him.

So if managing our Wealth Assets can make us successful, can those assets be mismanaged?

I think this question can be answered by looking at individuals who have lost the wealth inherited from their parents. These individuals have gone in reverse from success to situations of bankruptcy or the like. For example: The Eatons in Canada, while still living good personal lifestyles, were at the helm of the demise of a Canadian institution, and are headed in the wrong financial direction. I wonder if this was somewhat due to bad timing. Perhaps it was due to the fact that the surviving family members mismanaged their own Wealth

Assets? Did they forget what made their families successful: relationships and reputation? Some would say the Kennedys in the United States might be on the same declining path.

All financial wealth is a result of these Five Wealth Assets. This is how wealth is created in the first place. The balance, or relationship, between each of these Wealth Assets is your Wealth Equation. It is unique for each of us, because for each of us, the relationship is different; therefore, your formula for success is defined by and unique to you.

This is key: Financial wealth does not "just happen" for most of us. It is actually an outcome of well-managed Wealth Assets.

Wealth As The Product of Habits

I want you to think about this:

If the world's financial wealth were redistributed equally among the entire population what would happen?

My theory is that it would flow back to its originators over time. Why? Because wealth does not start with the accumulation of money. The creation of wealth is the result of activities and habits.

Our habits begin to be established from the time we are born — we absorb information from our parents, our siblings, then school, part-time and full time work. We invest a lot of time and effort into establishing those habits - albeit the effort is subconscious. Many of the habits we encumber ourselves with are not habits we would choose to embed, were we given a choice. We take them on because it's what we know, or experience. And if we had different advice, we might choose to work differently. So even though we start out with the same raw material, the way we construct ourselves, how we use what we've been given determines our level of success.

This explains why some people can create great financial wealth, lose it and create it again. In fact, the same habits that allow us to make wealth happen are not necessarily the habits we must use to preserve wealth. So some individuals excel at creating wealth, only to lose it because they don't understand stewardship — how to preserve and multiply what they have created.

Others are skilled at preserving wealth but don't understand what it takes to create wealth; therefore they are challenged in creating more.

Learning the habits that make wealth happen will make you rich beyond your dreams — because you have what it takes to repeat your success. You can do it over and over again, and find someone who is good at preservation to manage your wealth for you. It's easier to turn that responsibility over to someone else when you have confidence in knowing that you can re-establish your position if necessary.

I have found three habits that are essential to make wealth happen, and I call these the Three Success Ingredients:

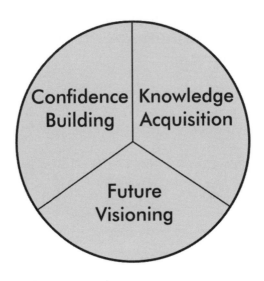

As you can no doubt see, these habits are all within our power to establish, increase, fine tune and perfect, if only we choose to do so. Each of us possesses these habits to some greater or lesser degree. The issue is: How often do you use, practice and grow them? Think of them as muscles; they become stronger with use.

The corollary is that many of us have habits that not only do not contribute to wealth, but that contribute to wealth reduction. We either have good habits, or bad habits — I prefer to call them aligned habits/non-aligned habits - each area as powerful as the other when used on a regular basis.

But they are only habits. The non-aligned habits can be replaced with habits that are in alignment with your vision. Equally important to note is that the aligned habits can slowly change to non-aligned or destructive habits if we do not stay focused on our vision.

So the advice I give you in the following pages is to identify the habits that align with your vision, establish them and practice them in your daily activities. Keep focused on those habits as you begin to become successful, keep doing what you're good at, and find someone to assist you in preserving the wealth you have become expert at creating. If you commit to doing this, you will achieve your picture of a life of wealth and success.

We're All Successful

Each of us is successful in our own world.

We all have the same assets with which to work, and we each have our own definition of wealth. We have established a set of habits and activities that serve us. Thus, we are successful in our own world. We are exactly where we are, given the parameters set out above. We have what we set out to generate.

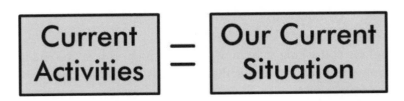

Where we are today is a direct result of the actions we have taken in the past, and our future will be based on the actions we take today. Thus we are successful. Each of us is currently achieving what we set out to achieve, whether it was intentional or not. Therefore we all have success. It may not look the way we envisioned it would because our current activities or habits won't take us on the path to that vision, but we are realizing the fruit of our current activities in a big way. And if we look to the past and see where we have been, compare it to where we are now, we have had some progressive success.

It's not for anyone else to judge our success. Our own definition of wealth and success is the only relevant definition. Moreover, there is no way to compare your success with anyone else. The only way to determine success is to measure your progress over a set period of time — looking for improvement and accomplishment, and comparing your current status with the goal of your picture of success.

The only measurement of success is comparing the current situation to a goal. YOURS! How close are you to reaching your definition of wealth? Are you meeting the timeline you set for yourself? Yes? Then YOU are having success, and that success is not measured by anyone else's standards.

One person's definition of wealth will be another person's failure. By this, I mean the individual who defines wealth as a monetary income stream and sacrifices everything for a pay cheque could be considered a failure by the individual who defines wealth by the amount of time they spend with their family. So the measurement of wealth and success is as individual as are you and I. I don't measure my success according to the standards of the world. I measure my success based on who I am now and who I want to be.

I can hear you asking right now, "So if each of us is successful in our own world of wealth, why is there such dissatisfaction among North Americans?"

The popular view is that the media is responsible for much of the dissatisfaction we experience. I don't believe this to be true. The media reports what is true for people. While they may arguably skew the reporting in one way or another and prey on our areas of sensitivity and vulnerability, I don't believe that the media creates dissatisfaction. We choose to believe what we choose to believe.

I believe that the dissatisfaction we see in North American society comes from two things: measurement and comparison.

The tools we use to measure success don't serve us well. Individuals tend to measure their success against their picture of success — their ideal or dream. They compare their current situation to the end goal, and get discouraged thanks to our culture of instant gratification. "Life would be better if I had a bigger house, more money, a better car. Life would be better if I could travel more, have more spare time, be financially secure. But I'm not there yet, so I'm failing. And it looks like I'll never get there."

Imagine if we measured where we are today, and looked behind us to where we've been. "Last quarter, this was my position. Last year I was here. Five years ago, this is what I had. And look where I am now! Wow!" We should be measuring our progress and how we've changed, not how far we are from the goal.

Have you ever taken a long road trip? There you are driving down a long straight road; you can see the pinpoint that's your destination way up ahead, and as you drive, hour after hour, it doesn't seem to get any closer. But when you look down at the odometer, you find you've driven hundreds of miles — how much closer you are to your goal! And knowing that you've traveled that distance gives you confidence. You know that if you continue on the same path, you will easily be able to reach your goal. The past gives us a frame of reference for the future.

Interestingly, as we move toward our vision for the future our perception of our accomplishments, combined with our experience, may even cause that dream to change! How much bigger can we dream when we see the success we're having now? How much greater is our possibility? Really it is just a matter of choice. You choose the perspective filter: not good enough or on my way.

The other dissatisfier is the way we compare ourselves to others. If we have defined wealth as it is for us, and if we know that no two definitions are the same, what, then, is the basis for comparison? We can't compare apples to oranges, or vast monetary wealth to the richness of uncommitted time. Yet this is where the media plays upon our uncertainties. We not only listen to media hype about the rich and famous of the world, and peek into their lives through our celebrity voyeurism culture, but we believe the advertising thrust upon us by the manufacturers of financial services and products who imply that we 'should' accomplish a particular definition of wealth and financial security within a set time period. I'm amazed at the amount of stress individuals experience trying to achieve something that may not even be applicable to them. I have met many individuals who have reached their definition of wealth, but who wouldn't dream of adopting the lifestyle portrayed through advertising. They'd go crazy doing nothing but playing golf and having breakfast on the terrace! They intend to be productive well into their senior years. I've met others who stressed themselves attempting to achieve that goal, only to find their successful achievement empty of satisfaction — because the end result was incongruent with their true picture of success. I had a client who had dreamed of retirement and travel. After six months of travel he came into my office and said, "Enough of that. I need a purpose beyond which buffet to eat at, now what do I do?" My response? "Consider it a sabbatical; now find a way to contribute again, but on your own terms".

This is key: Measure progress against actual results, keep the goal in front of you, and don't compare your picture or your present circumstances to that of anyone else.

Chapter 2

Old World vs. New World

What's wrong with this picture? We have more available to us now than any other generation in history. We have increased our standard of living. We have created time saving appliances, prepared foods, yard care services - all designed to give us more leisure time.

We have expanded the options for recreational activity - fitness clubs, sports arenas, league teams for summer and winter, extreme activities such as bungee jumping, parachuting and white water rafting. Travel tours advertise any kind of adventure - from glacier exploration to archaeological digs to casino cruises.

We have carved out more discretionary time, and then we have created more activities to fill the time we have created. We feel guilty while we just sit and relax — the frantic pace that life has become is pushing us faster toward dissatisfaction than it did our fathers and mothers and their parents before them. Our expectations of self and others far exceed what our ancestors experienced.

We are all successful in our own world.

Why, then, are we dissatisfied with our lives?

Why is the divorce rate in North America over fifty percent? Why are we encountering so much stress-related illness?

In North America, the standard of living is high. The average income has increased steadily over time. We live in a democratic society, safe from political unrest and oppression, unlikely to be torn by war, famine or universal poverty. We have health care and education available for all. We live in the richest part of the world.

Why the dissatisfaction?

I believe that our dissatisfaction is a disconnect between what we have been educated to believe and where the New World is at. A disconnect between Old World beliefs and New World beliefs. It's not just a generation bias; it is a paradigm shift.

it's a paradigm shift

Listen to the story of an immigrant family. Where they have come from doesn't really matter - it could be Italy, Portugal, Germany, the Ukraine, Poland, or South Asia - in fact, it could be the country of your ancestors. Their stories are the same — coming to the Americas for another chance, a new life, a place where opportunity knocks and everyone who works hard becomes successful.

John came to America after the war. (John could be Jean, Jack, Gianni, Jaroslav, Joe, Janal or Jakri) He came with a hope for a new life, with more opportunity for success. In the small town where John came from, there were few jobs, and it was difficult to support a family. So his brother, who came to America earlier, and has some room at home that he is willing to share, has sponsored John and his family. John is excited about the prospect of new opportunity. He has a great work ethic and is willing to do whatever it takes to give his wife and children the kind of life they deserve. John arrives and applies for several jobs, finally finding a job as a bricklayer for a construction company. The pay is minimal, and the hours are long, but John is able to support his family and contribute to the costs of his brother's home. Over time, John saves enough money to purchase a small home of his own. The children have to share their bedrooms, but it's in a safe neighbourhood, and the neighbours are friendly — some even come from the same small town where John grew up. Everyone looks after everyone else. They share what they have. They gather together for weddings, and funerals, and impromptu chats at night on the front step.

They all agree that you can only count on two things — death and taxes. Everything else depends on hard work and dedication. John trades his time for money, saves what he can, and is committed to giving his children a brighter future. An easier life, one where they won't have to worry about where the rent money is coming from. John works hard so his children won't have to. He doesn't want them to experience what he has. They will go to school, get a good education, get a good job, work in an office. They won't get their hands dirty. They'll work with their minds. And so John gets up at five every morning except Sunday, and trudges off to his job, knowing that the backbreaking work is the means to a richer life for his kids.

Chapter 2: Old World vs. New World

John Jr. and his brothers and sisters grow up watching their parents work. They let themselves in the door after school, do their homework and watch TV until their mother gets home from work and starts dinner. John arrives home and sits down at the dinner table to a hot meal with his family. The kids get part time jobs as soon as they're old enough, and swear that their kids will never have to work. John Jr. goes to college, gets a great job with a starting salary three times what his father makes after twenty five years of hard work.

John Jr. marries, buys a home in the suburbs and has a family of his own. He works as an office manager, studies at night to get accreditation in his field, and spends time with his kids on the weekend, if he doesn't have too much work. Johnny, his oldest, is registered in baseball and hockey, and has the latest and best equipment available. Mom's a hockey mom, driving the team to all the games and keeping score. Dad hardly ever makes a game, but when he does, he's demanding, pushing his son to go harder, faster. John Jr. believes that he's setting an example for his son - work hard at school, get a good education and get a good job - that's the measure of success. Johnny just wants his dad to throw the ball in the backyard.

Johnny graduates from high school, then college, and takes on a position in the accounting department of a large manufacturing company. He works from nine to five, and goes straight home to spend time with his kids. After his wife finishes her maternity leave and goes back to work, Johnny takes parental leave to be home during the "formative years". He has turned down two promotions because he's not willing to move his family to another city. Johnny is actively involved in coaching his daughter's soccer team, and is a volunteer with the local fire department.

The story of three generations - Old World versus New World. Each generation passes down their thoughts of how things work in the world — the grandfather believes in hard work for work's sake. Father believes that work is money and money is success. And the son values personal time — work is a way of earning enough money to buy enough time to be home. And each generation believes that their ethic is the one to follow.

What if each generation were right?

Because the world doesn't work the way it did in 1950, or even 1980 for that matter. Things are different. Times have changed. The pace of life has become more hectic. Technology has created new forms of leisure and new demands at work. We are walking through life looking in the rear view mirror — focused on where we have been and measuring where we are going against what we know for sure — past performance.

We must change our thinking in order to move forward; this means leaving some of our generational beliefs behind.

Each generation passes down beliefs, ethics, culture, values acquired from their parents and grandparents, and these are embedded in how we live and do business. It is interesting to look at the way we view these generational values as young people. Every generation says to themselves, "I'll never treat my kids that way!" or, "Things will change when I'm in charge!" And in fact, things do change.

I witnessed exactly this generationally contained thinking recently in a conversation with my own Grey Generation mother. She shared a story about her Gen X employee who was lamenting about not being satisfied at work. My mom summed it up by saying "Who does she think she is? Doesn't she know it is not about enjoyment, does she think we have been dragging our butts to work everyday for enjoyment?" I had a smirk on my Baby Boomer face when I saw it playing out in my own family. Let me explain.

Generation G, the Grey Generation - those born before 1940 — believed in honour, consistency, value. They played by the rules, and they made the rules. They were dedicated and worked hard. They made sacrifices for success, and they believed in conformity — toe the line, don't rock the boat, that's not the way it's done around here. Success and security were built on consistency.

The Baby Boomers followed — those born after World War II. They saw huge growth and expansion in all aspects of the economy. Growth was built on cooperation, collaboration. The early boomers were workaholics — ambitious and idealistic. The later boomers became materialistic — they saw what could be acquired through the spoils of hard work. These were the "yuppies", young upwardly mobile professionals. They were a little cynical about the rewards of good work habits and a positive mental attitude — they believed "it's not what you know, it's who you know."

Johnny is a Generation X — born after 1965. He wants his work to matter, and his work relationships to be positive. More important than opportunity for promotion and wages becomes job satisfaction and recognition of a job well done. Johnny gets overlooked, lost in the mix — the Boomers still dominate the work force, and there's little hope for the Generation X worker to climb the corporate ladder at the same rate as his or her father or mother. Generation X is technology oriented — they can adapt easily to changes, and there's a generation lap, not a generation gap, when it comes to technology. They work to live; they expect flexible hours and autonomy. They want to have fun at work, and prefer non-traditional roles and environments.

Johnny's kids will be part of Generation Y, affectionately known as Generation "Why?" More than 50% belong to one-parent families. They are the service providers, and will take care of the Greys and the Baby Boomers, both financially and physically. Gen Yers are environmental advocates — while the Boomers and the Xers used and abused the environment, the Whys see the need for global responsibility. And this is the first generation to have girls equally involved in education, sports and careers.

Right now, the largest group of individuals are the Baby Boomers like John Jr. He struggles with the old beliefs that his parents brought to

America with them, "get a good education, get a good job, then retire at age 60". And he doesn't fully understand the New World belief. He is caught in the middle between his father and his son. He has always been focused not on the value of work and the work ethic, but on what he can buy with the money earned. He is only now beginning to realize that he may not have sufficient funds to retire at age 60 as he has been led to believe. He is stressed out, in poor health and starting to question the things he has been told all his life.

Still, he can always earn more. What he knows for sure is that he will always be more successful than his parents. His son Johnny, who grew up with the same beliefs and family teachings — "get a good education, a good job and retire at age 60" — is also beginning to feel the same stress. Johnny is realizing that his generation, Gen X, is the first generation for whom there is no guarantee that their success will exceed that of their parents. He, like his father, is living life as described by Charles J. Sykes, author of the book, *Dumbing Down Our Kids: Why American Children Feel Good About themselves But Can't Read, Write, Or Add, Griffin, 1996*:

1. **Life is not fair - get used to it!**
2. **The world won't care about your self-esteem. The world will expect you to accomplish something BEFORE you feel good about yourself.**
3. **You will NOT make $60,000 a year right out of high school. You won't be a vice-president with a car phone until you earn both.**
4. **If you think your teacher is tough, wait until you get a boss.**
5. **Flipping burgers is not beneath your dignity. Your grandparents had a different word for burger flipping - they called it opportunity.**
6. **If you mess up, it's not your parents' fault, so don't whine about your mistakes, learn from them.**
7. **Before you were born, your parents weren't as boring as they are now. They got that way from paying your bills,**

cleaning your clothes and listening to you talk about how cool you thought you were.

8. Your school may have done away with winners and losers, but life HAS NOT. In some schools they have abolished failing grades and they'll give you as MANY TIMES as you want to get the right answer. This doesn't bear the slightest resemblance to ANYTHING in real life.

9. Life is not divided into semesters. You don't get summers off and very few employers are interested in helping you FIND YOURSELF. Do that on your own time.

10. Television is NOT real life. In real life people actually have to leave the coffee shop and go to jobs.

11. Be nice to nerds. Chances are you'll end up working for one.

Mr. Sykes wanted to communicate his version of reality to these youths about to enter life. He regrets that feel-good, politically correct teachings created a generation of kids with no concept of reality and who have been set up for failure in the real world.

And so the clash between Old World and New World begins, and we find ourselves in the middle of a conflict we don't understand. I hope to assist you in understanding the difference between these two worlds and how you can take advantage of this conflict.

The Wealth Equation

This concept has been used intuitively in different forms for centuries. It continues to be used by those individuals who consider themselves wealthy, a small group in our society. I have turned it into an easily understood formula for the rest of us to utilize.

The Wealth Equation is the formula for making wealth happen.

5 x 3 = results

wealth assets   success ingredients

By actively tweaking the elements within the formula you will be able to achieve your definition of wealth.

The Wealth Equation is the path away from Old World and into New World thinking about making wealth happen.

Times have changed. Old World thinking is not going to work in today's environment. People are living longer and requiring more resources as they age. There is more stress on health care, pension funds, and a greater pressure for self-reliance.

Wealth, whatever your definition, is elusive — it changes and morphs as you get closer to making it a reality. What looks like the definition of wealth for an individual just out of school, earning a full-time income for the first time, seems like a struggle to an individual at the peak of his career, with three children, a house, a cottage and university tuition to pay. The Wealth Equation serves both definitions equally well because we have come to understand that wealth is not about quantity and numbers, it is about abundance of your desired lifestyle. It is the quality of life that you live while in the pursuit of wealth as well as in the preservation of wealth.

Wealth flourishes as a result of the proactive management of your Five Wealth Assets: Health, Time, Wisdom, Relationships and Reputation. Your current wealth, as you define it, is a direct result of the attention you pay to these Five Wealth Assets. As with any assets, they need to be cared for, invested in, and appreciated on a regular basis. In fact the only way to move towards your ideal definition of wealth, attention to the development of these assets is critical.

Everything you have now, you have created through the use of these Five Wealth Assets.

Picture this: today you arrived home and every material thing you had was gone. The house, the car, the bank accounts — all gone! Could you replace all of that if you had good health, lots of time, the wisdom you have acquired and the relationships and reputation you have established? My guess would be yes.

You see everything you have is because of these five things. Without your health, you would at best be extremely challenged. Yet you also need strong, supportive relationships and a quality reputation in addition to time and wisdom. Your Five Wealth Assets work together synergistically to create wealth. The way in which you apply the ingredients — the factors impacting those assets: Confidence, Future Visioning and Knowledge Acquisition — determine the degree to which you acquire wealth.

The results you are generating today are coming from the utilization of your Five Wealth Assets. If you aren't getting what you want, you need to start changing things. And I can hear you protesting now! "What am I doing wrong? How do I best use my Five Wealth Assets?" Let's look at each of the assets as they relate to Old World thinking, and how the application of New World thinking will be more relevant in today's society.

Health

Here are some familiar words that reflect Old World Thinking:

- Play while you are young, because you'll spend the rest of our life working.
- You only see the doctor when you are sick.
- Work hard to make enough money so you can have fun.
- Life is hard and then you die.

Old World thinking has us squeezed into a mold that shapes the way we "should" live out our years here on earth. From the ages of 0 to 20, we play hard and have fun — no responsibility, just self-development, growth and maturing. Once we reach the age of majority, life is over as we know it — we become contributing members of society and we focus our energy on work, not play. We work long hours, bring work home, travel for work, and accumulate on a weekly, daily, hourly basis all the stress involved in performing to the standard set by our parents and our grandparents. Stress that eventually causes us to become ill.

When we finally reach the age of 65, we're forced to retire. The advertising myth makes that retirement even more attractive at the age of 55. Doesn't that sound good? If I can escape all this stress, I'll pull out as soon as possible. Then I can have fun and play through my retirement years. Except that we're too old and sick to enjoy it! The average police officer collects 18 pension checks after retiring from active duty. How much stress must be endured through his or her working life to cause the illness that eventually takes them away from that well deserved retirement? Is this what we are living for?

The Old World says that once you graduate from school, it's time to get serious and get a job. You can play when you retire. No wonder some people end up as perpetual students!

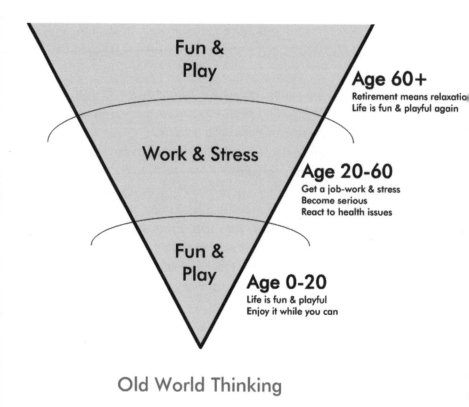

Fun & Play

Age 60+
Retirement means relaxation
Life is fun & playful again

Work & Stress

Age 20-60
Get a job-work & stress
Become serious
React to health issues

Fun & Play

Age 0-20
Life is fun & playful
Enjoy it while you can

Old World Thinking

New World thinking turns that concept around by breaking the mold. Why do we have to wait until we're old and retired to have fun? Why not make fun and play a lifelong goal? The inclusion of fun and play in our lives reduces our levels of stress. In fact, one of the treatments for many illnesses is comedy — laughter has been proven to be physically healing.

And why do we only pay attention to our bodies when there's something wrong? Students at medical school get virtually no training in vitamin and nutritional supplement use. Why not? What could be better than illness prevention? Imagine how rich life could be if we were all proactive in matters of health — nutrition, exercise, supplementation. If we were able to take measures to prevent the illnesses that killed our parents and grandparents, how much more rewarding would our life with our own grandchildren be? New World thinking suggests that we manage our health instead of managing our sickness. If life were balanced for us - if we had a balance between work and play, and if we could integrate play into work — the risk of illness would be decimated. Your health is an asset you cannot live without. As medical technology improves more and more rapidly, we are destined to live longer. Why not choose to live in a healthy body and a healthy mind? It has been said that when you are working at what you love to do, you never work another day in your life. Why not measure your life on goals achieved, rather than on chronological stage and age. If you didn't know how old you were, how old would you be? Think about it!

New World thinking causes us to want access to proactive healthcare. The fastest growing healthcare industry is alternative and preventative medicine, closely followed by extended care institutions for seniors. Government programs in Canada and HMOs in the United States are still operating within the Old World model. Both systems in North America are beginning to fail. The universal health care system in Canada does provide health care for all. Try accessing it! Waiting lists are long. Those without financial means receive the minimum care required; those with the financial means are leaving the country to receive care elsewhere. The Canadian system does an excellent job of emergency treatment. The American system has great access - no waiting lists, and individuals can buy the services needed, but the costs are out of control. The American system is user pay — you get what you pay for. It's a conundrum — the Canadian system has minimal cost to the individual with poor access to health care, and the American system has great access to health care at high cost.

The Old World model tells the individual how much health care they can receive, and caps the income levels of the health care workers. This model cannot last; we have not yet fully realized the implications of reactionary health care in North America. With the huge number of baby boomers on health care plans, the system is destined to collapse.

The Old World health system is reactive, postponing the inevitable. "The doctor knows best". "The government (or your HMO) will take care of you." Yet even now, many preventative services such as physiotherapy, chiropractic and eye examinations are being delisted from the services that the government health care system in Canada is willing to provide. The universal health care policy is morphing into a two-tiered system, with those who are willing and able to pay receiving better and more proactive health care than those who cannot.

In the New World, there is a focus on nutrition, on physical exercise and conditioning, on mental wellness and preventative care, with the biggest growth area being physical maintenance. Much like a car, we need to replace the worn parts to keep ourselves on the road. New hips, knees, hearts, kidneys, and whatever other replacement parts modern science can create. We know about and do something about proactive healthcare to mitigate the reactive care:

> A proactive physical approach focuses on aerobic, anaerobic and strength training to ensure acceptable cholesterol and blood pressure levels, and sufficient core body strength to maintain balance and bone mass.

> A proactive approach to nutrition emphasizes quality foods, no additives or toxic chemicals and nutritional supplements.

> A proactive approach to mental health recognizes that spiritual wholeness and self-help and motivational messages can do as much or more than physical intervention in both preventing and treating illness.

> And preventative care from a proactive approach means embracing new technology, regular examinations and scans for early detection of potentially harmful disease and illness.

All of this would be costly, but once instituted, could not only reduce and minimize the soaring cost of health care for the elderly, but could hugely impact life expectancy.

And even if the New World health care thinking is a long way off, you and I can be responsible for the choices we make regarding health care. Everything we've talked about is available to you and me. How we take advantage of proactive health care is our choice.

How are you managing Wealth Asset #1 - your health?

Exercise - write your answers to these questions in the space provided:

Health Definition:

How would your time on earth improve if you had great health?

How would your wisdom improve if your had great health?

How would your relationships improve if you had great health?

How would your reputation improve if you had great health?

What is your personal definition of health?

Why is your health important you?

What is your personal definition of health?

Look at your activities and their outcomes, both short and long term

Some Health Equation examples:

Smoking = Shorten life span
Occasional poor quality food = reduced short term energy
Long term poor quality food = reduced life span
Exercise = longevity
Balanced diet = longevity

Occasional drink = no impact
Heavy drinking = reduced life span and quality of life
What is your current Health Equation?

Time

Sixty seconds in one minute. Sixty minutes in one hour. One hundred and sixty eight hours in a week. Four weeks in one month. Month after month after month; season after season; winter, spring, summer, and fall. The rhythm of time passes unnoticed until we suddenly turn around and look behind us. How did we miss what has passed by, while we were busy doing?

Time is our most precious asset. It cannot be replaced. Once time is gone, it cannot be retrieved. In order to get the most from this asset, you must guard it jealously, protect it against the thieves who try to steal it - time wasters that come in disguise. Telephone calls that could be postponed. Urgent matters that could be delegated. Television shows that could be recorded to be watched later.

When someone tells you, "I don't have time", they're showing you their true priorities. Each of us has the same amount of time, and we can choose to spend it foolishly or we can choose to spend it wisely. If we examine the way we spend our precious hours, it's interesting to note that we seem to have the time to do the things we truly want to do, the things that are most important to us. And the "no time" excuse is used to avoid the things we want to do the least.

34

The significant thing about time is that it never changes — it's the one thing that is predictable — we know exactly how much we have and when we will get it. So the task of time management is really a misnomer. We don't really manage time; we manage the events that we choose to fill our time. Where we actually spend our time is the best clue to the truth of our habits.

It really comes down to choice — how do you choose to spend your time? Ask yourself every day — "Is there something else I would prefer to be doing right now?"

If there is, why aren't you doing it? Life is short. Time is precious. Time is wealth.

Old World thinking says that an individual is free until it's time to attend school. Once in school, teachers, parents and homework control our time. When we reach the point where we become contributing members of society by securing employment, we sell our time to the highest bidder, over and over again. Finally, at the age of 60 or 65, when we retire, we own our own time again.

The New World has different expectations — the Old World model doesn't work anymore. Today's generations value their time and their ownership of that time. Great conflicts arise for the worker's in today's corporate environments. Remember Charles Sykes' speech. This generation wants balance between home and work. This generation has values that embrace family commitments and obligations and which are as important as the work ethic of their grandparents.

There is great conflict in corporate North America today. Companies try to accommodate the needs of Generation X and Generation Y by offering a repackaging of the corporate workday — flex time, work from home, child-care facilities in the workplace, job-sharing, sabbatical programs. All these measures are designed to ease the burden of the New World worker and reduce time-related stress. The outcome? People have more leisure time, which they then fill up with other organized activities that put a strain on their scheduling and on their time. And the technology that freed us from the hours of overtime spent at work now connects us 24-7. We are working more — we can't shut off our brains! We're tied to that Pavlovian response — if the telephone rings, we have to answer it. And now, with the convenience of Blackberry technology — e-mail is on our hip, to be responded to at the first hint of vibration — and we can't leave it alone. Our time is no longer our own.

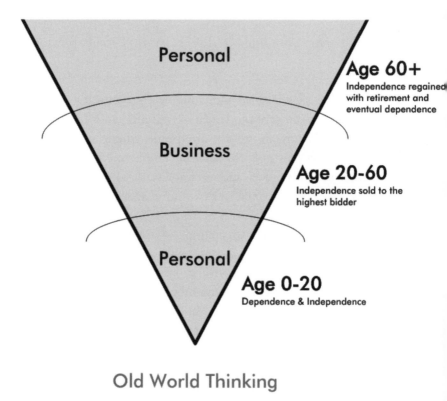

Personal

Age 60+
Independence regained with retirement and eventual dependence

Business

Age 20-60
Independence sold to the highest bidder

Personal

Age 0-20
Dependence & Independence

Old World Thinking

No wonder we all long for retirement. Old World thinking treasures the 0-20 years and reminisces about the freedom of childhood. After age 20, your life is not your own — your employer owns and controls you until every drop of effort is squeezed out, just like the empty toothpaste tube. Retirement is the only escape; in the Old World, no one thinks of working past retirement age. Financially, this creates pressure on us to save while we work so we can spend in retirement. And with the failing health of corporate pension plans and social security programs, that saving may in fact be for survival. Many people are finding that they can't afford to retire — they look back over their life and realize just how much quality time was wasted chasing the fantasy of luxurious retirement.

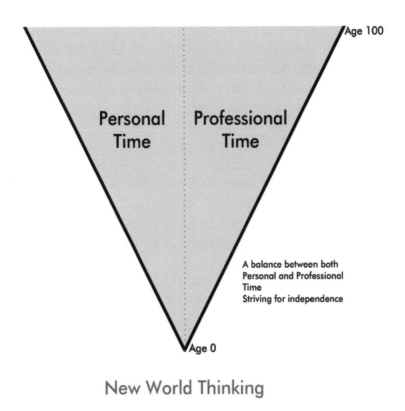

New World Thinking

In the New World, our life is balanced between professional and personal activities. We work to live, instead of living to work. We are living longer now than ever before. We have been spending that time racing through our productive years with no sideways glance at the opportunities passing us by. That's an interesting phrase, isn't it? We "spend" our time — just like it's money! Yet we don't cherish our time to nearly the same degree that we cherish our money.

Why not enjoy the journey? The correct balance of personal and professional time is unique to each individual and to each family. Most of us, if asked, would say that the one thing that's missing in our lives is more personal time. Imagine a life where you were doing a job you loved to do, and had time to spend with family and friends, enjoying the richness of relationships. Opportunities pass. A missed opportunity to spend time on a picnic, or in a sailboat, or at the theatre won't cost much in the moment. But what possibilities could have opened up for connection with family, for appreciation for nature or the arts, for the creation of memories in the instant that we choose obligation or comfort over a new experience?

Picture an entire life spent on great personal time and great work time. In the New World, we understand that if we live a long, healthy, profitable life, doing the things we love to do at work and at home, we will never have to stop. We won't long for retirement. We won't long for things to be different. And we won't suffer the pressure of having to bankroll a huge amount of money in preparation for retirement!

When your life is satisfying and rewarding, when you have the time to do those things that feed your soul as well as your body — your picture of what you need is significantly altered, and your need for material things diminishes in proportion to that level of satisfaction.

Our grandparents enjoyed the satisfaction of working hard. And when they came home from work, they spent their time with family and friends, creating rich and rewarding networks. Remember Leave It To Beaver? Father Knows Best? Ozzie and Harriet? While we have come a long way in liberating women from those stereotyped roles, what attracts us to those fictional depictions of family life is balance. They had balance. There seemed to be an uncomplicated simplicity and focus in their lives that we yearn for today.

Their children, our parents, have created the nuclear family — removed in distance from family and friends. Busy with meetings, business trips, kids' extracurricular lessons and teams, dinners eaten standing up or in the car, rushing to the next thing. In the pursuit of a richer lifestyle, they have lost the ability to be alone. To be creative in unstructured time. To just stop and sit and notice the rhythm of the world they are in.

It's now time for us to take back our time. To honour our personal needs as much as our need for success in the professional arena. To give ourselves time to grow and flourish intellectually, spiritually, and interpersonally; to create memories for our families; to build the legacy we truly want to leave — not simply a massive portfolio of stocks and certificates of deposit, but the legacy of honour and respect and memory that only time well spent with people can create.

It is amazing the clarity of focus one can achieve when you recognize that growing a well-loved and guided child is far more valuable than growing a huge inheritance for a child. It sets the boundaries in terms of attention for creating the financial wealth component. It is not wealth at the stake of the child it is wealth for the sake of the child.

In the end we must take control of our priorities and our ownership of time. We must be focused. The amount of time available is set; our activities can and must align in order to move forward, whatever our definition of wealth.

Never, ever forget Einstein's definition of insanity - doing the same thing over and over expecting a different result. If you want to change some things in your life, you have to change some things in your life. Change starts with looking at what you are doing.

How are you utilizing your time?

Exercise - write your answers to these questions in the space provided:

Time Defined:

How would your health improve if you had great time management?

How would your wisdom improve if your had great time management?

How would your relationships improve if you had great time management?

How would your reputation improve if you had great time management?

Why is your time important to you?

What is your personal definition of time?

Look at your activities and their outcomes, both short and long term

Some equation examples:

Always late = broken commitments, hurt feelings, lack of dependability, hurts reputation
Allowing interruptions = missed deadlines, offensiveness, disrespectful

Scheduled time = tasks accomplished

Planned recreation time = stress reduction, improved performance, extended life span, better health

Flexibility = stress reduction, efficiency

What are your current Time equations?

| |
| |
| |
| |

Wisdom

I met a man of seventy years in a local coffee shop. I asked if I could share his table and we sat in companionable silence for a while. He started a conversation by making some astute observations about some of the other patrons of the shop, and I was surprised at his insight. Wanting to know more about him, I asked a few questions. This remarkable man had traveled every continent while conducting his business. He had a large family, all of who lived within driving distance, and whom he saw regularly. He had written articles for several trade magazines, and had recently dabbled in the popular press. Well-read, intelligent, experienced — what a wonderful resource he could be! And when I asked him who was benefiting from all his wisdom, he replied, "Oh, no-one wants to hear from an old has-been. The younger folks with more energy have all the influence. I'm just an old man who can't keep up with the new way of thinking."

How sad that he would so think, but what a truism about our lack of respect for the wisdom of experience.

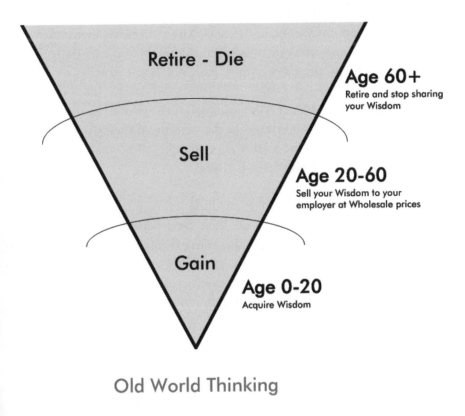

Old World Thinking

In the Old World, we acquired wisdom from the time we were born, through the school years up to twenty, and then leveraged our wisdom in the working world, selling it, expanding it, continually acquiring it, until the moment we retired at age sixty. What happened to all that wisdom? It was wasted on the old, no longer valuable.

What do we do with sixty years of wisdom at retirement? We golf. We garden. We live in a retirement home in Florida for the winter, and on the lake in the summer. We have been sold that this is what the golden years are all about.

Yet the most satisfied retirees are those who don't. Successful people don't stop using their wisdom — they can't. They've been doing it for 60 years and they enjoy it. It's become a rewarding habit. So they look for avenues to share their wisdom — either they continue to work in their chosen environment, or they share it in new environments — volunteer work, mission work, consulting. Sharing wisdom doesn't have to end — there's no expiry date, no "best before".

The majority of North Americans sell their wisdom to their employers at wholesale. Employers take the wisdom of their workers, repackage it, and sell it to the market at retail prices. Who makes the money? Not the wise workers, that's for sure!

Most financially successful individuals leverage their wisdom directly to the retail market. They do their own packaging, marketing and promotion. And they reap the rewards themselves — there's no middleman to take the profit of their hard earned wisdom. And although they might describe themselves as business owners, in reality, they are self-employed. If your definition of wealth includes financial wealth, take a look at the Forbes 500 list of wealthiest individuals. Few of these are employees — most are self-employed or at least have an ownership stake, selling their wisdom at retail.

The most successful individuals have discovered their unique talent, and that is what they work on, grow, and then leverage. Unique talent is that thing we all do that no one taught us — it is innate, it comes naturally. We may have learned the skill of refining it, but the talent lies within us. For some, that talent is obvious. For others, it may take work to identify.

Sometimes we watch small children performing tasks and we wonder, "How in the world did they ever learn to do that?" The answer lies in their unique talent. Our job is to allow that talent to foster and grow. Unfortunately, the Old World interferes with the way we do our job.

When you were growing up, did you ever hear someone tell you, "Get a good education so you can get a good job — then you'll earn enough money to enjoy your retirement?" The Old World myth rears its head.

We send our children off to get a formal education where every child is treated the same, taught the same, measured the same and pushed out the door expected to think the same. There is very little focus on individual skill and talent. Memorization and rote skills are rewarded — independent thought is frowned upon. The child's unique talent is pushed down until it smothers from lack of stimulation. I'm amazed at the number of successful individuals who left school early due to a lack of excitement, challenge and stimulation; we see it every day.

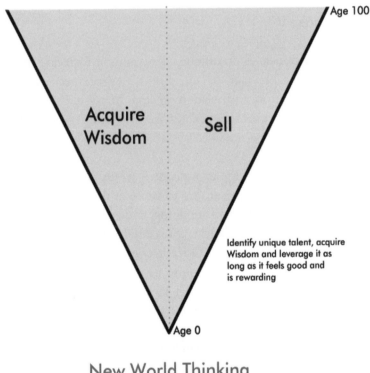

Age 100

Acquire Wisdom

Sell

Identify unique talent, acquire Wisdom and leverage it as long as it feels good and is rewarding

Age 0

New World Thinking

The New World is changing all that. That credo doesn't apply any longer — no one is guaranteed a good job, regardless of the level of education. People with master's degrees are driving cabs, or working on the assembly line. We're not really sure what a good job is — our definitions are changing as rapidly as our need for balance — a good job is no longer defined by salary or benefits — it may be defined by flexibility, opportunity for advancement, or the ability to choose our own path.

The New World at work is centred on individuality. More and more children are being home-schooled — learning through distance education and focusing studies on their particular interests, their unique talents. Learning environments are tailored to the individual, and coming out of that learning environment is an individual with huge expectations for professional performance that don't fit Old World thinking.

The New World focuses on unique talent, and on fostering that talent regardless of age or stage of life. Life now becomes a journey of knowledge acquisition and wisdom selling. Many individuals, young and old, start businesses to leverage their wisdom. Age is no longer a factor.

I've never understood why an individual would learn and grow for forty years, and then stop learning to retire at the peak of his or her wisdom. If you love what you are doing, and are making a good living at it, why stop? Is it due to external pressure from the media expounding the virtues of retirement? Does it come from the thousands of investment advisors who want you to invest in retirement portfolios? All of this pressure to retire and take life easy doesn't make sense from a practical standpoint. Work for forty years, then stop and spend the next thirty years in leisure. A human being needs a reason to get up in the morning. That purpose in life that we search for through our "middle age" doesn't evaporate on retirement.

What will happen in North America over the next ten years with the millions of Baby Boomers voluntarily retiring and/or being forced to retire? What will we as a society do about that loss of wisdom? Major corporations experienced this brain drain in the downsizing trend of the late 80's and early 90's. In order to reduce payroll, the core wisdom of the organization was gutted, and what remained was a company with no culture, no experience and no wisdom. What will the retiring individuals do when they retire? Golf? Garden? Those senior years are some of the most productive — what a waste! And what will they live on? The stats are terrifying; most North Americans do not even have the financial means to retire at the time they are forced to leave.

In order to achieve your goal of wealth, it is imperative for you to take ownership of your wisdom. If you own your own home, you take care of it. Each week you mow your yard, tend your garden, and maintain and repair. Go to any Home Depot on a weekend — the store is crammed with homeowners honouring the responsibility of good home stewardship.

Yet, we do not treat our wisdom the same way. Wisdom is our greatest asset; it is the asset that created the "dividends" to purchase the home and keep it current and fresh. How much have you invested in your wisdom? It is responsible for providing everything you have. Don't take it for granted.

When was the last time you did something to improve yourself? When have you asked yourself, "How can I better utilize my wisdom and talent? How can I sell my wisdom and talent on a retail basis? How can I eliminate the middleman? Or at least reduce his cut?"

Our purpose and talent is still alive; it was there when we were young and we haven't lost anything — we just need to make an investment, just like the house down the street that needs a little tender loving care. Start investing today and reap the rewards in the future. Knowing that you have created what you have today through your wisdom, what would your future look like if you made a big investment in wisdom? It's almost beyond imagination. It's an unprecedented future, your future and your future uniquely alone — one that has never happened before.

Think about it — everything you have today has been created by the utilization of your wisdom. You earned dollars in exchange for wisdom. What would your future be like with a greater investment into your wisdom? How much more valuable would your wisdom be? Why do you think companies pay for job-related education and training? As you become more knowledgeable and experienced, you become more valuable - they get more profit through your work.

We need to invest in ourselves. Many individuals who invest in mutual funds or something similar would be very happy with a rate of return of ten percent over the long run. Twelve percent would be great. But what would your rate of return be if you spent $10,000 on upgrading your wisdom? What type of payback would you get over the long run? What would it look like if, instead of renovating your house for $100,000, you went to Harvard for a year? What return on investment would that give you over your lifetime?

Many individuals do not have a plan for investing in their wisdom. Most of us haven't even thought about it, but this is the key to success. You must invest in the areas that give you the greatest wealth, whatever that looks like.

Exercise - write your answers to these questions in the space provided:

Wisdom Defined:

How would your health improve if you grew your wisdom?

How would your time on earth improve if you grew your wisdom?

How would your relationships improve if you grew your wisdom?

How would your reputation improve if you grew your wisdom?

Why is your wisdom important to you?

Chapter 2: Old World vs. New World

What is your personal definition of wisdom?

Look at your activities and their outcomes, both short and long term

Some equation examples:

Self employment = freedom, fear, excitement, autonomy, control
Job = security, boredom, controlled, compromise
Media - paper and electronic = information
Internet = data
Formal schooling = knowledge
Coaching/mentoring = wisdom
Books = data, information, knowledge
Experience = wisdom
Newspaper = current events
Great books = wisdom
Reality TV = recreation

What is your current wisdom equation?

Relationships

Relationships are the centre of the human experience. While I include all types of relationships family, friends, business, I would be remiss if I did not place the largest emphasis on family relationships. That is where it all begins and where it is all modeled. And this statistic saddens me a great deal:

> "Presently 40 percent of first marriages in this country end in divorce. 60 percent of second marriages and 75 percent of third marriages end the same way. Apparently the prospect of a happier marriage the second and third time around is not substantial."
> *Gary Chapman, in The Five Love Languages (Northfield Publishing, 2004)*

The importance of relationships has fallen dramatically for most North Americans. We do not put value on our relationships. This has been an increasing trend over the past fifty years. As we pursue success and the almighty dollar, family values have taken a back seat. We rationalize that we are serving our families by creating a "lifestyle" for them — a life of material goods that substitute for our presence in their lives. Do you know how I spell "rationalize"? "Rational lies" — lies we tell ourselves to make it okay to miss our son's soccer game, to cover up forgetting an anniversary, to give ourselves permission to be thoughtless and selfish in the interest of getting ahead.

With the pursuit of material goods and lifestyle, we have allowed relationship failure to become acceptable. Lack of connection not only affects the adults in our life, but the children as well. What will our society be like forty to fifty years from now if we continue to downgrade the importance of relationships? We are willing to invest a great quantity of time and money into peripheral things like jobs and the material trappings of success. Yet, when it comes to investing in relationships, it appears that we are on the verge of bankruptcy.

In the Old World, we were taught that money would make us happy.

A great job would make us happy. Marry a good man and he will take care of you. Get a good education and you will be able to provide for your family. Few people said, "Your spouse is the most important person in your life; make him or her your number one priority. Your children need your time, wisdom and guidance; make them a priority. Your friends and other family members need to be priorities." Instead we were told to buy a house, get a car and save for retirement. Lots of time for relationships later! Unfortunately, by then there's no one left with whom to spend your time.

New World thinking prioritizes work and personal lives in equal balance. Work is important for self-fulfillment, for financial success and for professional growth and development. And quality time with family and friends relieves stress, eases tension and allows for a ripening of relationships. New World thinking realizes that the pressure to perform is self-induced. No one ever lay on their deathbed wishing they had spent more time at work. Most people looking back on their lives wish for a slower pace, fewer demands on self, more time just being in the moment, appreciating what is rather than chasing after what might never be.

It strikes me as significant that the two most important letters in the words "human beings" are 'b' and 'e'. We are human "be"ings, not human "do"ings. Yet we spend our time focused on what to do and how to do it. Do, have, be. If we work hard in school and get a good education, we will have a good job and we will be successful. I heard that when I was growing up; I'm sure you did, too. In fact, I would wager that you're telling your own children the same thing.

Yet if we think of all the great leaders, successful people in the world, not one of them was focused as much on what they were "doing" as they were on their way of "being". Each of them — Winston Churchill, Mother Theresa, Nelson Mandela to name a few — had a vision of how things could be in the world, and set out to make that vision a reality. Each leader was a visionary, focused, determined, unwavering, committed, dedicated, inspiring, confident … and all the other adjectives that describe great leadership. They were "being" this way in every thing they "did". The "doing" was physical evidence of the "being". They were "being" inspirational, and what they were "doing" communicated their vision, so they "had" followers who joined them on their visionary journey. "Be — Do — Have".

It is the law of sowing and reaping. If we sow watermelon seeds, it is fruitless to expect tomatoes to grow — we'll get watermelons, and nothing can change that fact. So it goes with our way of being — if we sow selfishness, isolation, lack of connection, what will we reap when we get old and the harvest is ready? Don't expect to see friends and family waiting at the end of that road to embrace us and celebrate who we have been throughout our life. We will reap loneliness, isolation and lack of connection.

But if we sow consideration, time, respect, connection, availability, willingness to serve, then what will we reap at the end of the day? We will experience others who respect us, who are connected, who are available to share their precious time with us.

What a simple formula, yet how difficult to follow given our culture of bigger, better, more!

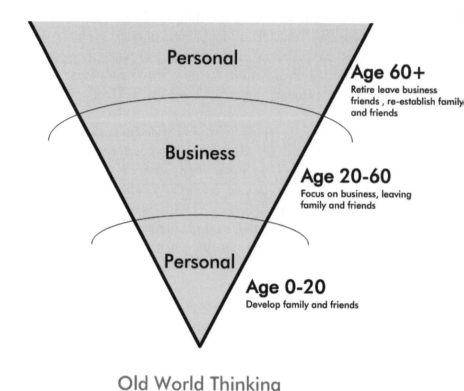

Old World Thinking

Old World thinking kept us at work, on overtime, nose to the grindstone, and when we were home, we were thinking about work. Family time fit into the blank spaces. We lived with family until age twenty, then entered the business world and adopted a new family — colleagues, bosses — we totally focused on business relationships. We thought our families and friends would always be waiting for us. After all, family is where you go when no one else will take you in. In nurturing our work relationships in order to get ahead, we failed to feed our personal relationships. Our families learned to live without us. Our spouses left us, and our children moved out. If there was actually someone waiting when we finally came home, that person was a stranger to us. Life had been all about work and dealing with the kids, and now when there are just the two of us, we have nothing in common. In the Old World, marriages survived out of inertia — what is at rest tends to stay at rest; it was often easier just to keep the status quo. What a sad story of a wasted life! And how long does it take for our business relationships to fade? Just try this experiment — get a pail of water, and stick your arm into it as deep as it will go. Now pull it out. Is there a space left where your arm was? Noooooo! The water moved in to fill the space you took up — and that's about how long it will take for someone to move into your office and change the nameplate. Within a few months, you will be obsolete — so out of the current race that you couldn't come back if you tried.

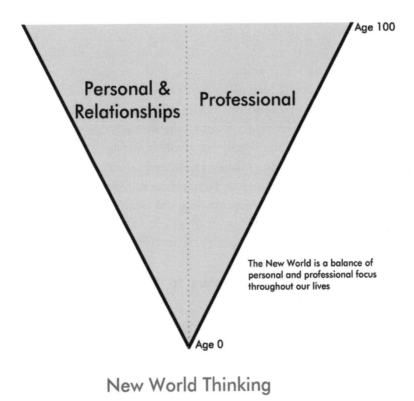

New World Thinking

The New World leader is committed to rich, rewarding relationships at home and at work, in a healthy balance. We want to be totally engaged in what's happening for our spouses, our children, our parents, siblings, and all of our friends. They are our support network

— they're whom we call on in the darkest of moments, and we are equally there when they need us. And at work, we have our support team also — those people whom we trust, can have meaningful and productive conflict with, who commit to decisions and are accountable, and who focus on team results. And we have relationships with our clients — we adopt a servant mentality — we seek an answer to the question, "How can I help?" We create loyalty through relationship, and enjoy the referrals we engender through this way of being. Daniel Goleman, in his book, Emotional Intelligence, Harvard Business School Press, 1996, writes that the two reasons smart people fail are an inability to manage change and an inability to manage relationships.

Relationships and the ability to tend and nourish are the fourth Wealth Asset that will help us to create wealth. In formal training and educational curriculum, no one is taught how to have better relationships on a personal level. Everything I've ever learned was self-taught — trial and error — and boy, those errors sure taught me what not to do! Don't make the same mistakes time and time again; invest in your knowledge of relationships; protect and encourage the people around you and they will assist you in creating the wealth you seek.

Exercise - write your answers to these questions in the space provided:

Relationships Defined:

How would your health improve if you had better relationships?

| |
| |
| |
| |

How would your time on earth improve if you had better relationships?

How would your wisdom improve if you had better relationships?

How would your reputation improve if you had better relationships?

Why are relationships important to you?

What is your personal definition of relationships?

Look at your activities and their outcomes, both short and long term

Some equation examples:

Regular dates with your spouse = love, attention, longer life expectancy

Irritability = reduced communication, offence

Quality time = greater communication, feeling of well-being, stress reduction

Communication = clearer understanding

Controlling relationship = withdrawal, lack of communication

What are your current Relationship equations?

Reputation

Are you willing to give up your reputation in order to make a buck? Are you willing to be known for a quick tryst in the office?

It appears that many North Americans are willing. They must be willing because we hear of it happening time and time again. In the past several years, we have seen many business leaders and political leaders sacrifice their reputation in order to gain.

Do you remember Enron and their accountants? How about WorldCom? And Martha Stewart chose to serve her five-month jail sentence for insider trading "to get it over with", rather than await the results of an appeal. Why? Is it a power play? Is it greed? Both? Or is it because they feel invincible? And there's no such thing as bad publicity — bad press is good for the papers and better than no press at all.

In the Old World, our reputation was tied to what we were doing at that specific time. As a student in high school, you longed to become the best — athlete of the year, valedictorian, prom queen — you wanted to be popular.

Once you started working, your occupation became your identity. When people asked you to introduce yourself, they wanted to know what you did for a living, and you wanted to tell them. I'm a doctor, a mechanic, a police officer, a baker — as if the identity created the vision of success. Once you retired, you became a retired doctor or mechanic, and you became a retiree, a senior, a snowbird. This was your reputation. It was established by who you were at work — no mention of "I'm a husband, a wife, a father, a mother, a grandparent, a volunteer, a skier, a sailor, a woodcarver."

What image do you have when you hear the term, "stay at home mother"? Even today, that phrase evokes confrontation and debate. Some see it as the most important job in the world — others see a non-contributing member of society — what a true disconnect! And what a challenge for those who believe that they can have both; they don't want to choose between the roles.

Desire for success can lead us to places we never thought we'd go — we've forgotten about the importance of reputation.

Yet reputation is core to our success — people who don't know us personally will judge us by what they've heard. When you apply for a promotion or a new position, you can be certain that your reputation will be one of the first things explored to see if you're a fit for the new job. When police officers are hired, the recruiter will visit the applicant's sibling's place of work to ask about the applicant. And then, the recruiter will hang around until the sibling takes a break, then enter the workplace and ask the co-workers what the sibling has said about the applicant — looking for reputation.

Individuals are running around with designer suits, luxury cars and large mortgages while their children are latchkey kids — left to their own devices. People will leave their children with strangers, but they won't let anyone drive their new car. It's as if the image makes the person, rather than the person leaving a lasting impression through reputation.

In the New World, we look at reputation beyond the trappings of success — beyond the suits and the cars and the houses. Values become the important measure. Character and the evidence of character become key to assessing reputation. The New World is based on a defined set of values that we manage and build upon. It's interesting that most people will say that honesty for them is a highly held value, yet they admit to cheating on their income tax.

But this is the original sin. People get caught up in the excitement of the moment and make choices that ultimately ruin their reputations. And those "rational lies" kick in — everyone else is doing it, so it must be okay. I won't get caught — no one will ever know. It's just this one time. The problem's not so bad that I can't fix it. And the most dangerous lie of all — if I cover it up, no one will know that I made a mistake. How sad that people don't have enough character to own up to their mistakes! People will more easily forgive a mistake than they ever will an attempt to deceive. Just ask former U.S. President Bill Clinton!

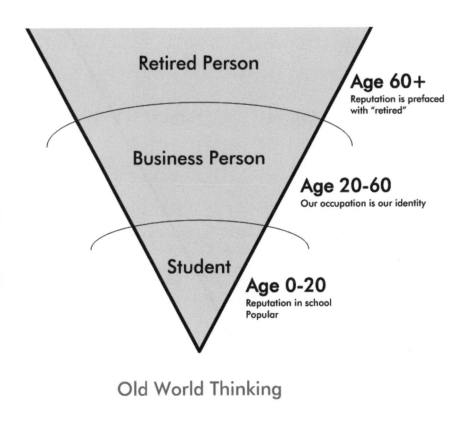

Old World Thinking

Old World reputation was based on what you did and where you were in life. Judgment was made about who you were based on external evidence. If you drove a big car and lived on the right side of the tracks, you were successful. And you could screw up as long as you didn't embarrass anyone superior to you in the organization. You didn't really manage your reputation; it just existed, based on what you did for a living. The challenge with that inevitability is that a reputation attached to a career evokes the lowest common perception of that career. We all know the stereotypes about used car salespeople and lawyers. But I know some very good people who happen to earn a living being a lawyer or selling used cars. Do you want your reputation to be based on derogatory stereotypes reflecting what you choose to work at? Do you engage in judgment?

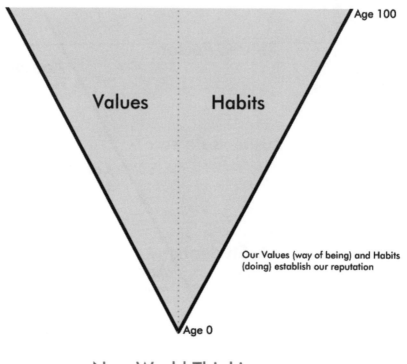

New World Thinking

In the New World, we can create a vision of how we want the world to see us. And that vision is based on our values and how well we can be true to those values as we wade through the day-to-day temptations to waver.

Ralph Waldo Emerson said that what we do speaks so loudly that what we say can't be heard. So we create a set of habits that help us to act with integrity, to walk the talk, to follow the vision we've created for ourselves, our goals and our purpose. And we establish a reputation based on our way of being and the habits we practice. That reputation is what carries us from successful interaction to successful interaction. From good performance rewarded by profit to referrals from clients pleased with our service. And if we stay focused on our vision, focused on our purpose and maintain the habits that serve that vision, we will never let our families, our business associates and ourselves down.

Values Exercise - What do you value most? How are these values consistent with the way you act? Do you do what you say? Do you walk the talk? How do they reflect on your current reputation?

Identify Your Values
Choose the ten values listed on the next page that are the most important to you. Remember that each word is uniquely interpreted by the reader, so choose what's significant for you, not what you think it should be or what others might choose. There are some blank spaces to insert values that are significant for you but not listed here.

☐achievement	☐excellence	☐profitability
☐caring	☐fairness	☐quality
☐caution	☐family	☐quantity
☐challenge	☐flexibility	☐relationships
☐communication	☐freedom	☐respect
☐compassion	☐fun	☐responsibility
☐competition	☐growth	☐risk
☐cooperation	☐honesty	☐security
☐courage	☐individualism	☐service to others
☐creativity	☐innovation	☐speed
☐curiosity	☐integrity	☐task focus
☐customer focus	☐involvement	☐teamwork
☐determination	☐learning	☐trust
☐diversity	☐organization	☐uniqueness
☐empathy	☐positive attitude	☐winning
☐enthusiasm	☐productivity	

Now list your values in order of priority from most important to least important. Are these the values you're willing to stand for in your life? What future do you want to create?

1	6
2	7
3	8
4	9
5	10

Exercise - write your answers to these questions in the space provided:

Reputation Defined:

How would your health improve if you had a better reputation?

How would your time on earth improve if you had a better reputation?

How would your wisdom improve if you had a better reputation?

How would your relationships improve if you had a better reputation?

Why is your reputation important to you?

What are the 3 most important characteristics I should have?

What is your personal definition of reputation?

Look at your activities and their outcomes, both short and long term

Some equation examples:

Show up on time = respect for others
Show up late = I'm more important
Finish what you start = trust
Steal = thief
Listen = care
Self promotion = arrogance
Do the right thing = ethical

What are your current Reputation equations?

Chapter 3: Success vs. Greater Success

Chapter 3

Success vs. Greater Success

The Three Success Ingredients

So, what separates success from greater success? If each of us is successful in our own world, and if we all begin with the same Five Wealth Assets, what separates the Oprah Winfreys of the world from the rest of us?

I propose that there are three ingredients that create success. The degree to which you apply each ingredient today determines your ultimate level of success.

The three ingredients? Confidence, Future Visioning, and Knowledge Acquisition.

We all use these ingredients every day. Unfortunately, because we haven't identified them as key to our success, we often don't use them in a focused manner, and we don't use them in equal proportions.

Imagine that you have three people working on an assembly line, assembling three-part widgets. Each performs a different but essential task, and each person's performance is key to the successful delivery of the widgets to the customer. Now imagine that one of the workers has been working very hard, producing her portion of the widget. She decides to work some overtime, and has accumulated a surplus of widget parts — so many that her work station is overflowing and she has no more room to work. That overproduction puts pressure on the other two widget-makers to produce, and they also start to work overtime, trying to keep up. This could work in the short run, increasing production and profit. But over the long run, such behaviour is bound to create problems. What happens when one of the widget-makers books off sick, or takes a two-week vacation? Widget parts pile up and production stops. Manufacturing of widgets requires consistent behaviour over the long run. In the short term, a fluctuation can be managed; in the long run, balance of widget part production is essential to continued success.

It's the same with the Three Success Ingredients. We've all met someone who exudes confidence, but is lacking in vision and knowledge. In the short term, that confidence will work when connecting with people, creating openings for further interaction and possible business transactions. However, what happens over the long run? Their lack of knowledge about their business, and their lack of vision about their purpose will show up, and the clients will move on.

Unbalanced Success Ingredients

Another commonly occurring example is the individual who is technically sound, but lacks the confidence to make connections or contact. While they are astute in their cognitive skills, their success is limited to their ability to establish relationships.

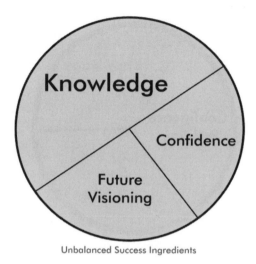

Unbalanced Success Ingredients

Finally, I'm reminded of the story of the ploughing match. In a ploughing match, the farmer who ploughs the straightest furrow wins the match. So how does one plough a straight furrow? Not by looking behind at where the tractor has been! The straightest furrow comes from the farmer who looks ahead to the fencepost at the end of the field - his goal, his destination. Without a vision of where I'm going, all the confidence and knowledge in the world will not get me there. If I don't know where I'm going, any road will take me there!

Confidence!

Being confident means daring to dream! It means making decisions and taking risks! Confidence means self-esteem and self-worth. You deserve your wealth.

Balanced Success Ingredients

Most individuals let lack of confidence hold them back. The interesting part is that fear and lack of confidence live only in their heads. It is not what is so, but what we believe to be so. If you think you can, or if you think you can't, either way you're right!

It's amazing how our minds play tricks on us. In lacking confidence, we are susceptible to "awfulizing" — creating in our minds awful consequences out of the unexpected turns and twists of day-to-day activities. Rather than seeking more information, we tend to "make stuff up" about ourselves and our success.

How many times have you said to yourself, "I could have done that."? "What's he/she got that I don't have?" "What makes them better than me?" "I had that idea — why didn't I say anything?" "I wish I could do that." Is your lack of confidence letting you down?

Many individuals are very successful only because they have the confidence to ask for something. This happens every day in every business.

72

Why is Joe the salesperson able to meet with an important prospect? He had the confidence to call and book the appointment. He felt self-worth; he believed he was worthy of the individual's time and business.

If you ask someone like Joe how he does it, his answer is simple. The worst thing that can happen is that the prospect says no. Joe's self-esteem and confidence is not hurt or destroyed. The prospect said no to the sale, not to Joe. And most likely, Joe got another name, a lead or a referral from the individual who said no. Joe is confident in his product and his ability to sell. The prospect just wasn't buying.

Your confidence grows through measuring progress on a regular basis, much like a sports athlete measures his or her success. Confidence builds as we move forward and the only way to know how far and how fast we are moving is to track our progress. Measure your performance against targets and goals set frequently and regularly, and you will feel more confident.

Future Visioning:

Your future is only as big as the vision you have created. The greatest contributor to greater success is setting great, big, hairy goals.

Balanced Success Ingredients

Goal setting allows you to take advantage of opportunity. People who are lucky are those who are prepared when the opportunity arises. I believe that opportunity is everywhere; you will only attract the opportunities you set out to experience. For example, if your goal is to set up a home based business to get some tax advantages and pay off some debts, that's exactly what you will get. If your goal is to set up a major company generating $1,000,000 annually, you will also succeed. The size of the goal changes our mindset and attracts the opportunities.

The Harvard School of Business studied a graduating class of MBA students, surveying them to discover whether they had set goals, and whether those goals were written. Approximately thirty percent had set goals, and five percent had actually written down their goals. A follow up interview thirty years later showed that of the graduating class, the thirty percent who had set goals had achieved some, if not all, of those goals set thirty years prior. And the five percent who had written goals had not only achieved all of their goals, but they were financially worth more that the remainder of the graduating class combined.

The power of goal setting is unsurpassed as a vehicle for success. And once the goal is set, the brain goes into action, searching for opportunities based on what you've told it to do — the goals. Thus, the individual who merely wants a home based business will only identify the opportunities to support that goal, whereas the individual who wants to create a major corporation will identify the opportunities needed to reach that goal.

Try out this simple exercise to demonstrate the power of your brain. Visualize your favourite car. Think about what colour you'd like, the options you would choose, and visualize yourself driving that vehicle. Now pay attention to what you notice over the next couple of weeks.

I think you'll find that your brain goes to work, searching for vehicles that match your picture of success. Imagine! If we can harness the power of our brain to identify the car we'd like to drive, what could we do if we actually focused on the success of achieving our goals!

A word of caution! Do not confuse dreaming with goals or goal setting. Many North Americans dream of being financially wealthy and retiring yet are doing nothing specific to move them in that direction. A dream is not a goal. A goal is something you have authority or control over, specific in nature and with a planned set of activities that lead to its achievement. It has a measuring system to determine progress. Dreaming is essential to the visioning process, but the dream is not the goal. A goal is action-based; a dream has no road map.

Here's how to tell if a goal is big enough. It must have an element of both fear and excitement.

My definition of a great goal — "It scares the poop out of me, yet I get so excited by the idea I idea I could pee myself." A little crude, perhaps, but the best description I can give for how I feel when I set a big, hairy, audacious goal.

Do your goals have an element of fear and excitement? Think back to all the great events or parts of your life — your first day of school terrified you, yet you wouldn't want to miss it! When you got your first job — fear and excitement. The delivery of your first child — fear and excitement. They're always present for the big accomplishments — if your goal doesn't have both fear and excitement, you will not move forward.

Perhaps my most recent experience will illustrate this — Halloween was an exciting prospect for my three and a half year old son, Luca. For the three days before Halloween, that's all he talked about. Halloween was Sunday, and he didn't eat all day — he told us he was waiting for his candy.

Our neighbours across the street began decorating on Saturday morning — they always go all out, creating a big, scary display. Luca watched with interest, and this was the first house to which he wanted to go. As we walked up the driveway he looked nervous, and said he had changed his mind — he'd rather go to another house. Off we went. We visited maybe twenty houses — some with displays, others with just a pumpkin.

By the eighteenth house Luca's confidence had grown. At one house without decorations, he told me that big boys only go to the scary houses. He didn't want to go to this house — it wasn't scary enough. "Where would you like to go then?", I asked him. "Back to the first house; I'm a big boy", was his reply. He went through the display, which was very noisy and scary. He came out beaming and proud. He had a big scary goal and he achieved it. He just needed to build his confidence first, and that's what he did. When we got home, he had breakfast, lunch and supper, all in the form of chips and candy.

Overcoming fear with excitement and accomplishment is just about the best fertilizer you can find for growing your assets!

Knowledge Acquisition:

Knowledge is the tool that separates us from the other mammals on the earth. We are able to gain, retain and redistribute our knowledge.

Balanced Success Ingredients

Knowledge is based on reading, gathering information and storing experiences. An individual with knowledge learns as much from failure as he or she does from success.

Successful individuals pursue life-long learning. These individuals know what they are good at, and can identify what others are good at. They pursue knowledge with an interest and they pursue wisdom with a passion.

Knowledge includes understanding your capabilities. Many successful individuals would tell you that they are not the smartest people in the world, but they do have a clear understanding of how things work. They also know their purpose, and their unique talent, and they leverage their vision and their talent, understanding the value that they bring to the world. And knowledge isn't only about gathering and retaining information. It's also about discernment — knowing which nugget of information will work for you, and which one you can ignore. There are as many financial strategies as there are analysts willing to propose them — you will choose the one that's right for you. It's the same with knowledge — it's not all useful, so discard what you can't use and grab onto the stuff you need to propel you to further success. The key to knowledge acquisition is being able to decipher the difference between information and wisdom. For example, information comes from the newspaper or news broadcasts. Wisdom comes from many years of experience, from the application of knowledge. Wisdom lasts forever; information changes hourly. Many people read the newspaper and watch the news. But few read great books or expose themselves to unique experiences that allow them to obtain wisdom.

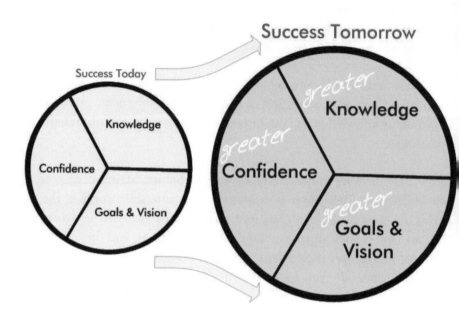

You already have some measure of success today, or you wouldn't be reading this book. You can credit that level of success to how you have applied, however subconsciously, the Three Success Ingredients.

In order to move to a greater success, you now need to tweak the formula. You need to multiply the size of your confidence, your goals and vision and increase your knowledge, and you will exponentially increase your level of success.

This is key: Create bigger goals, have more confidence, and share your wisdom with the world.

Chapter 4

Moving Forward

By now, you're probably saying to yourself, "That's all well and good, but how do I do it? What do I have to do to change, and to implement what Craig is talking about?"

First, get out of the Old World thinking. The entrepreneurial spirit that brought our great grandparents and our grandparents to North America has to be resurrected. Our forefathers left family and security in a familiar world for a new and frightening journey to a land of opportunity. They were willing to do whatever it took to create success, and they did. We've settled into a life of complacency, of satisfaction with mediocrity. Perhaps we have trapped ourselves with what we were told we needed to have and be.

Get out of Old World thinking

Reject that "settled for" life and break out the entrepreneurial spirit. Take risks! And if you fail, guess what? You get to go again. Henry Ford didn't create the Model T by giving up when he went bankrupt — more than once. Winston Churchill didn't give up when he was advised to surrender by his council during the Second World War. Nelson Mandela didn't give up during his 27 years of imprisonment while seeking reconciliation in South Africa. Ray Charles didn't give up despite growing up in poverty, having a long-term drug problem, being black during segregation in addition to being blind. His vision for his music helped him to overcome the many obstacles in his way — he had a vision for what people wanted to hear, and he had the confidence to ask for a contract that no one else had ever obtained — not even Frank Sinatra. The only difference between these leaders and you is the way they managed their Five Wealth Assets and Three Success Ingredients.

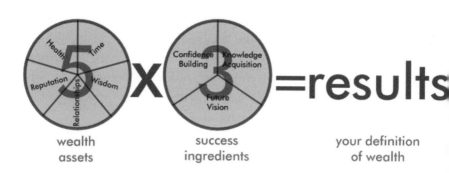

wealth assets × success ingredients = your definition of wealth

Second, define what wealth means to you - as an individual, then with your family included. Create a clear definition of wealth, outlining your philosophies and values on Health, Time, Wisdom, Relationships and Reputation. The exercises on the pages that follow will assist you in creating that clear definition. You'll be amazed at how your focus takes hold once you start to write.

Create a clear definition

Once you have a clear picture of the Five Wealth Assets and your definitions, you can then begin your journey to greater success. Remember, your level of success is dependent upon how you apply the Three Success Ingredients: Confidence, Future Visioning and Knowledge Acquisition.

The one common theme coming out of this is that you have to take ownership and control of your own future. If you're not in control, someone else is. What does this mean for you? It means being accountable for every aspect of your life.

And being accountable may mean leaving the corporate world or big government and moving out on your own — the self-employed businessperson. That's a huge risk — and the rewards are in proportion to the risk. Try it; you won't be disappointed. If you aren't ready to take that step right away you can still practice these concepts; expect some limitations to your success. And be warned, you will become increasingly frustrated with the Old World ways!

If you truly want greater success, take a look at how you can change what you're doing today to move you to greater ownership of your success. Be honest with yourself. You can't change what you don't own and you can't change what you don't own up to.

Using the exercises I've provided in the following pages, create a plan for moving forward that identifies your definition of wealth and success, that creates future visioning, that identifies knowledge acquisition requirements to achieve your goal, and that lays out specific tactics you'll need to take to move forward.

I strongly recommend that you find an accountability partner. This is someone who cares about your success, but for whom your success or lack thereof has no bearing on his or her own level of success. They would be responsible for holding you accountable to the goals you've set, the habits you're willing to create and the tactics you've identified to reach your goals. And, as the word "partner" implies, you would do the same for him or her.

The exercises use the Three Success Ingredients to assist you in moving yourself forward. After clearly defining what each of the Five Wealth Assets is for you, you will

1. Create a vision of how you see yourself 10 years, 5 years, 1 year, six months and one month from now in relation to that Wealth Asset,
2. Identify what is true for you today, and then compare your equations with your vision — identify new equations to close the gap, and
3. Create new habits by identifying the tactics you will use to move yourself forward.

By completing these exercises, you will be able to identify the flat spots in your process, and will create a dynamic self-improvement program that can only help propel you toward your future success.

Chapter 5

How to Create Your Future

All of the things we have talked about so far are interesting, and hopefully have awakened you to a new possible reality. But, this book promises to show you how to make wealth happen, so this is the section where you roll up your sleeves and lay out a plan with specific actions, so you may begin to do the work. That is how wealth happens, by knowing where you want to go, how to get there and then DOING IT consistently and continuously.

So let's get started with the doing.

As I discussed in the past chapters if you want a different future from your past you need to change some things. The big question that looms at the start of the process of making wealth happen is "What things need to change?" After all, you do not want to make changes for change sake and you want to take advantage of things you already do well, of which I am sure there are many.

You have already started the process if you have been completing the exercises at the end of the each of the Wealth Assets section. Those exercise sections provided you with a format for identifying what is important to you and also allowed you to start realizing and articulating your definition for each of the Five Wealth Assets. The worksheets following this chapter assist you in further focusing your definition of wealth and result in an action-oriented plan on how to make wealth happen by applying the Three Success Ingredients to the Five Wealth Assets.

It is a sequential process. First you define your ideal future, and then you do a "work back" of the steps you need to take between then and today. You do this for each of the Five Wealth Assets. You then do an honest inventory of what is standing in the way of making that happen, and that shows you what you need to work on. You will then pull all of the pieces together at the end, and that is your action plan — what you need to do to make wealth happen.

It is simple to explain, but not necessarily easy to do.

I have a couple of important comments to make about this process:

1. This is an iterative process. I hope that you will come back to this over time and update or adjust it to your current circumstances. As you move through this process you will become more and more aware of your needs and desires, this will help you to become more focused with every accomplishment. What seemed critical today may be less important in light of new competencies and discoveries you make during this process. Embrace the natural focusing outcome of the process and integrate into your plan.

2. Some find it difficult to even start because they are unsure or cannot picture their ideal. This is so important, just start with AN answer, rather than paralyzing yourself with the search for THE answer. I have seen people stall at the contemplation stage for weeks, months, even longer because they cannot see the ultimate future for themselves yet. This is a symptom of the state of confusion you may be currently mired in. Do not let it stop you. Pick a spot that is further out from where you are today, any spot. And work your way to it. Even the smallest steps achieved build immense confidence in your abilities and the process. When you have accomplished that, set another future goal, even bolder than the last time, and keep on going. Your consistent and continuous effort will get you

to your future, your steps can be large or small, that just affects timing.

Let me explain the process a bit more before you jump into the work sheets section.

The first step is to identify where you want to be - Future Visioning. Remember the future has not been created yet, so it can be anything you want it to be. For each wealth asset you will create a vision 10 years from now and then you will move towards today.

Next you will identify what is true for you about each wealth asset — Knowledge acquisition. You cannot move forward until you are true to yourself so be honest with yourself. This is the area that you will begin to uncover your wealth equations. Your current wealth equations compared to your future vision will identify the disconnects. The disconnects will show you the way.

Once you identify what is true for you can acquire the knowledge that will move you forward.

Let's go through one sheet together to give you an idea of how it works:

HEALTH

You will be able to answer this first question by looking at the answers to your exercises. Describe what health means to you.

My Health Definition: "Healthy to me means ......"

The second step is your ideal reality. When you are 10 years older than today, what does your future look like? Remember, you can make it whatever you want it to be, nobody else is going to (or should) draw the picture for you. Make it a picture that excites and motivates you.

Future visioning: "Ten years from today, my health will be …..."

This next section, picture yourself in the time frame indicated and itemize what the specifics look like, list as many as you can so that you can really see what it is.

Describe how you would like your health to be 10 years from today?
Describe how you would like your health to be 5 years from today?
Describe how you would like your health to be 3 years from today?
Describe how you would like your health to be 1 year from today?
Describe how you would like your health to be 6 months from today?
Describe how you would like your health to be 1 month from today?

This fourth step makes you face the reality of your situation today. Be truthful with yourself. Only when you are real can you see the disconnects from your future. The beauty of this step is that it reveals what work you need to do. At the end of this section you itemize your actions to take.

Knowledge Acquisition:
What is the current truth about your health?
What is the current truth about your Weight?
What is the current truth about your Nutrition?
What is the current truth about your current medical reports and analysis?
What is the current truth about your Physical - strength, anaerobic?
What is the current truth about your Mental, spiritual, motivational?

What are the major areas of disconnect between your current and future vision?

Who do you need to talk with in order to better align your current health to your future health?

Now that you have completed your future visioning and have completed your assessment of your current health your next step is to identify your current health equations. By this I mean the many small formulas or habits that either are aligned or not aligned with your new future. This is crucial as your equations will identify the habits you need to improve upon and the habits you need to eliminate.

What are my current Health Equations?
What are my new Health Equations?

Almost there! Now, write down the specific actions (tactics) you need to take and note beside it the date that you need to accomplish it. Then you need to choose the ones that you think are critical to making a difference / impact. Then prioritize the top three. It is important to narrow it down to 3 otherwise, the list of to do's will be overwhelming. You need a place to start.

Tactics: "I will ... by ..."
What are the specific actions you can take to ensure success?
What are the top 3 tactics to focus on for the next 12 months? What will you do about those three things, and by when will you do it?

Now do this for each of the Five Wealth Assets, and then pull them together at the end.

Chapter 5: How to Create Your Future

Chapter 6

Making it Happen

Building Confidence by Measuring Success:

It's important to measure your progress. How you measure it determines the speed at which you grow. Progress must be measured against the goal in small increments, and not against the dream. Remember that we discussed the difference between a dream and a goal. A dream is a fantasy; some thing that is not real. A goal is clearly and specifically identified.

That is why I want you to set out not only a long-term vision for your Five Wealth Assets, but also a short-term vision. Measure your progress against the short term.

Old world measurement - measures into the future (what you have not reached yet) but it has not taken place yet so how can you measure it? And if it has not taken place there is nothing to measure except an expectation of somthing that should of happened.

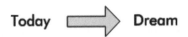

New world measurement tracks progress. It measures from where I am today to where I came from. It is inherently more rewarding and focuses on the progress made. You can actually see the progress and measure it against to goal. It has taken place.

Look at where my health is today as compared to last month. This will measure progress. This is very important for confidence building. Small steps lead to walking, walking leads to running. Confidence is the same. It takes small success to breed larger and larger ones.

Each successful step you take will build your confidence. Your achievement will be a result of your equation activities. Simply put, everything is action/reaction.

Exercise = longevity

Smoking = shortened life span

Align your activities with your goal. If you want a shorter life span, then smoke, eat poorly and do not exercise. Many sufferers of potentially terminal illnesses, in fact, do exactly that, trading quality of life for excess. These activities have been proven to shorten one's life span; if you want to accelerate the process, add drugs and alcohol to excess. This will improve your progress.

It's true that not many people have a goal to shorten their life span. Still, there are many who participate in the activities above with no concept of the future outcomes. Most people, if asked, would choose to lengthen the span of their life. The answer? Change your activities, change your equation. Reduce drug and alcohol intake. Eat properly, exercise and stop smoking. Live long and prosper.

Similarly, if you want financial freedom then you must define what that looks like for you and begin the activities that move you in that direction. Measure backwards against the short term, always looking forward to the long term. These short-term measurements will build confidence. Success breeds more success. Short-term measurements will also identify areas for improvement — wisdom acquisition. Short-term measurement provides clarity about what you are trying to achieve in the long term.

Worksheets

For each of the Five Wealth Assets, transfer the definitions and relationships from the other Wealth Assets into the space provided. Then use that information to assist you in Future Visioning, Knowledge Acquisition and using Tactics to create an Action Plan.

1
HEALTH

My Health Definition: "Healthy to me means …"

| |
| |
| |
| |

Future visioning: "Ten years from today, my health will be…"

| |
| |
| |
| |

Describe how you would like your health to be 10 years from today?

Describe how you would like your health to be 5 years from today?

Describe how you would like your health to be 3 years from today?

Describe how you would like your health to be 1 year from today?

Describe how you would like your health to be 6 months from today?

Describe how you would like your health to be 1 month from today?

Knowledge Acquisition: "Right now I look like this..."

What is the current truth about your health? — Weight

What is the current truth about your health? — Nutrition

What is the current truth about your health? — Current medical reports and analysis

What is the current truth about your health? — Physical: strength, anaerobic

What is the current truth about your health? —Mental, spiritual, motivational

What are the major areas of disconnect between your current and future vision?

Who do you need to talk with in order to better align your current health to your future health?

What are my current health Equations?

What are my new health Equations?

Tactics: "I will ... by ..."

What are the tactics you can take to ensure success?

What are the top 3 tactics to focus on for the next 12 months? What will you do about those three things, and by when will you do it?

2 TIME

Time Defined: "Time to me means ..."

Future visioning: "Ten years from today, I will spend my time..."

Describe how you would like to be spending your time 10 years from today?

Describe how you would like to be spending your time 5 years from today?

Describe how you would like to be spending your time 3 years from today?

Describe how you would like to be spending your time 1 year from today?

Describe how you would like to be spending your time 6 months from today?

Describe how you would like to be spending your time 1 month from today?

Knowledge Acquisition: "Right now I look like this…"

What is the current truth about your time management?

What is the current truth about your personal time?

What is the current truth about your spousal time?

What is the current truth about your children time?

What is the current truth about your family and friends time?

What is the current truth about your business time?

What is the current truth about your client time?

What is the current truth about your team members time?

What are the major areas of disconnect between your current and future vision?

Who do you need to talk with in order to better align your current time management to your future time management?

Who do you need to talk with in order to better align your current personal time?

Who do you need to talk with in order to better align your current spousal time?

Who do you need to talk with in order to better align your current children time?

Who do you need to talk with in order to better align your current family and friends time?

Who do you need to talk with in order to better align your current business time?

Who do you need to talk with in order to better align your current clients time?

Who do you need to talk with in order to better align your current team members time?

What are my current time Equations?

What are my new time Equations?

| |
| |
| |
| |

Tactics: "I will ... by ..."

| |
| |
| |
| |

What are the tactics you can take to ensure success?

| |
| |
| |
| |

What are the top 3 tactics to focus on for the next 12 months? What will you do about those three things, and by when will you do it?

| |
| |
| |
| |

3 WISDOM

Wisdom Defined: "Wisdom to me means ..."

Future visioning: "Ten years from today, I will be using my wisdom by..."

Describe how you would like to be using your wisdom 10 years from today?

Describe how you would like to be using your wisdom 5 years from today?

Describe how you would like to be using your wisdom 3 years from today?

Describe how you would like to be using your wisdom 1 year from today?

Describe how you would like to be using wisdom 6 months from today?

Describe how you would like to be using your wisdom 1 month from today?

Knowledge Acquisition: "Right now I look like this…"

What is your wisdom? What is the one thing you do that no one ever taught you?

How do you sell your wisdom: wholesale or retail?

How are you currently improving your wisdom?

If you were to ask 5 people, "What is my talent?", what would they tell you?

Identify 5 people and ask the question. Record your answers here

What are the major areas of disconnect between current and future vision?

Who do you need to talk with in order to better align your current wisdom to your future wisdom?

What are my current Wisdom Equations?

What are my new Wisdom Equations?

Tactics: "I will … by …"

What are the tactics you can take to ensure success?

What are the top 3 tactics to focus on for the next 12 months? What will you do about those three things, and by when will you do it?

4 RELATIONSHIPS

Relationships Defined: "Relationships to me are..."

What is your personal definition of relationships?

Future visioning: "Ten years from today, my relationships with....will be..."

Describe how you would like your relationships to be 10 years from today?

Describe how you would like your relationships to be 5 years from today?

Describe how you would like your relationships to be 3 years from today?

Describe how you would like your relationships to be 1 year from today?

Describe how you would like your relationships to be 6 months from today?

Describe how you would like your relationships to be 1 month from today?

Knowledge Acquisition: "Right now I look like this…"

What is the truth about your relationship with your self?

What is the truth about your relationship with your spouse?

What is the truth about your relationship with your children?

What is the truth about your relationship with family and friends?

What is the truth about your relationship with your business?

What is the truth about your relationship with your clients?

What is the truth about your relationship with your team members?

What are the major areas of disconnect between your current and future vision?

Who do you need to talk with in order to better align your current relationships to your future relationships?

What are my current Relationship Equations?

What are my new Relationship Equations?

Tactics: "I will ... by ..."

What are the tactics you can take to ensure success?

What are the top 3 tactics to focus on for the next 12 months? What will you do about those three things, and by when will you do it?

5 REPUTATION

Reputation Defined: "Reputation to me means ..."

"What are the 3 most important characteristics I should have?"

Future visioning: "Ten years from today, people will say I am..."

Describe how you would like your reputation to be 10 years from today?

Describe how you would like your reputation to be 5 years from today?

Describe how you would like your reputation to be 3 years from today?

Describe how you would like your reputation to be 1 year from today?

Describe how you would like your reputation to be 6 months from today?

Describe how you would like your reputation to be 1 month from today?

Knowledge Acquisition: "Right now I look like this..."

What is the truth about your reputation?

Describe your reputation.

If you were to ask 5 people, "What is my reputation?", what would they tell you?

Identify 5 people and ask the question. Record your answers here:

What are the major areas of disconnect between your current and future vision?

Who do you need to talk with in order to better align your current reputation to your future reputation?

What are my current Reputation Equations?

What are my new Reputation Equations?

Tactics: "I will … by …"

What are the tactics you can take to ensure success?

What are the top 3 tactics to focus on for the next 12 months? What will you do about those three things, and by when will you do it?

SUMMARY WORKSHEET

My overall definition of Wealth is

My Health definition is

My Time definition is

My Wisdom definition is

My Relationship definition is

My Reputation definition is

My 10 year goals are:

Health

Time

Wisdom

Relationships

Reputation

My 5 year goals are:

Health

Time

Wisdom

Relationships

Reputation

My 3 year goals are:

Health

Time

Wisdom

Relationships

Reputation

My 1 year goals are:

Health

Time

Wisdom

Relationships

Reputation

My 6 month goals are:

Health

Time

Wisdom

Relationships

Reputation

My 1 month goals are:

Health

Time

Wisdom

Relationships

Reputation

Final Thoughts

Thank you for reading my book, and for being willing to look at what's holding you back in your pursuit of making wealth happen. It is a brave and thoughtful thing you do! Once you take this path, there's no turning back - you know too much!!

Your feedback and comments would be greatly appreciated. The initial concept of writing a book was frightening — I have never attempted anything like this before. But big, hairy, audacious goals have both fear and excitement, right? The excitement of sharing what I have learned kept me moving to completion.

Your future is as big as the goals you declare. And your goals should be directly tied to your philosophies and values: your definition of wealth. Goals will change over time and accomplishment; your philosophies and the stand you take will stay true.

You are the wealth creator. Financial products can protect your family from the impact of uncontrollable events such as death, disability, inflation and taxation. They are only tools — they are not the wealth creators. You are what you say you are — wealthy — only if you act that way. Reinvent your future by recreating your habits. You are in control. There's no turning back!

Starting today, **Make Wealth Happen**.

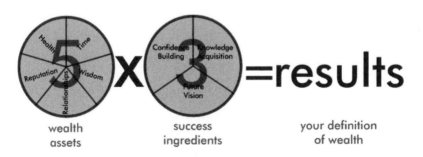

| wealth | success | your definition |
| assets | ingredients | of wealth |

Craig Matthews

Craig Matthews lives in Calgary Alberta with his wife of twenty years and their young son. In addition to authoring this book, Craig owns two companies, one of which is The Wealth Strategists, a wealth strategy boutique that inspired this book. He has worked with clients for many years and witnessed fascinating and highly personal variances in the definition of wealth. In his business he helps people articulate and live true to their own individual definition of wealth by helping them to understand their own philosophies and values.

Craig's personal wealth equation is founded upon a solid base of security, having the basics taken care of in a sensible, conservative way. This affords him the ability to indulge in opportunities as they present themselves. The most compelling opportunities for Craig come in the form of learning, time off with his family, travel, and business growth. Having designed his entrepreneurial business life to integrate with his personal life, he has been able to find a balance that results in quality attention and effort in both areas that keep him constantly rejuvenated, engaged, innovative and rewarded. As a result, Craig looks forward to actively contributing throughout his life to family, business and community.

For individual Wealth Equation consulting, group workshops or bulk book sales, contact:
www.makewealthhappen.ca
info@makewealthhappen.ca
403.543.1511